ONLINE
MARKETING
in 7 Days

First published in 2010 by Marshall Cavendish Business
An imprint of Marshall Cavendish International

5F / 32–38 Saffron Hill
London EC1N 8FH
United Kingdom

and

1 New Industrial Road
Singapore 536196
genrefsales@sg.marshallcavendish.com
www.marshallcavendish.com/genref

Marshall Cavendish is a trademark of Times Publishing Limited

Other Marshall Cavendish offices:
Marshall Cavendish International (Asia) Private Limited, 1 New Industrial Road, Singapore 536196
• Marshall Cavendish Corporation, 99 White Plains Road, Tarrytown NY 10591–9001, USA •
Marshall Cavendish International (Thailand) Co Ltd. 253 Asoke, 12th Floor, Sukhumvit 21 Road,
Klongtoey Nua, Wattana, Bangkok 10110, Thailand • Marshall Cavendish (Malaysia) Sdn Bhd,
Times Subang, Lot 46, Subang Hi-Tech Industrial Park, Batu Tiga, 40000 Shah Alam, Selangor Darul
Ehsan, Malaysia

A CIP record for this book is available from the British Library

ISBN 978-981-4328-19-7

Printed and bound in Great Britain by
TJ International Limited, Padstow, Cornwall

ONLINE MARKETING
in 7 Days

A PRACTICAL GUIDE FOR EVERYONE WHO CAN'T AVOID IT ANY LONGER!

Sarah McCartney

Marshall Cavendish
Business

CONTENTS

INTRODUCTION

ONCE IT WAS TRICKY, BUT NOW GETTING ONLINE IS EASY

In the late 90s and throughout the 00s, organisations realised that they needed websites. In the mid 90s, when under 5% of the UK's population had email, there were some amazing, groundbreaking sites. Some were built by enthusiasts for nothing, while others cost companies a fortune, when sought-after, skilled people built them from scratch.

There were also some appalling sites. Web developers could experiment with building whatever they liked, and they got away with it because most MDs and CEOs didn't have computers and had absolutely no clue what was being built in the name of their brands.

A virtual pub won design awards. These days, people laugh at the idea. What would be the point of that? You can't buy a drink there. But back then, people were just exploring the internet to see what they could make it do.

There were some great sites too. The team at Offworld Industries built the first ever website for city workers to order their sandwiches online; their choices came out as faxes at their favourite sandwich shops, and got delivered to their desks. That really did have a point, and the technology involved those days was groundbreaking. Offworld built it just to show what was possible.

One complaint was that companies would pay tens of thousands for their sites, then ask about the return on investment. They couldn't see that it was bringing in any business. "Where's the benefit to my bottom line?" they would ask, and they are still asking that now. But they could ask the same thing about all their marketing, online and in the real world.

So this book will concentrate on who your customers are, the best ways to bring them to your site, and what you want them to do when they get there.

Now, every business can benefit from being online. It's not as expensive as it was, and if you don't need anything too grand, you can create it yourself for less than the price of a pair of shoes. This book will get you going within a week; as long as you devote the time to it, there's every opportunity to be travelling along the information superhighway with the rest of the modern world.

If you do want something more grand, work through this book and you'll have a brief to hand over to your web designer and builder. (And if you are the MD or the CEO, you can also use it to help you keep up with what the kids are talking about in online strategy meetings.)

If you print a brochure or a catalogue, you don't leave it on your reception desk and hope that someone happens to drop by the office to collect one. If you build an online presence, you've got to bring people in to visit it.

WHAT'S STOPPING YOU?

There are two parts to getting your online marketing right:

- IT skills
- marketing skills

When I work with people who want to get started online, some have avoided it because they think they'll need to be IT experts. Their concerns are that it's going to be very complicated or expensive, or both, and secretly some of them believe that they'll get it wrong and make complete idiots of themselves. Often their uncertainty puts them in a position to be taken advantage of by people who might want to sell them something they don't need. Read on, and you'll learn enough to do it yourself or pay someone to do it properly without spending money on things you don't need.

The ones who are familiar with the internet and spend a lot of time using their computers, are really keen to jump straight in there and get going. But often they haven't done the marketing thinking.

- Most of them don't have the marketing knowledge to make their sites say the right things to their customers.
- They haven't thought about what their customers need and want to know.
- Some of them don't have to spend time on a website; a blog would be perfect for them.

- Others need to know how to brief a web design company to create the right site.
- Almost everyone needs advice on branding, and on copywriting in a way that suits their organisations.

The aim of this book is to take you through the thinking, planning and skills you need to start marketing your organisation online.

In a week.

HOW TO USE THIS BOOK

It's a workbook. To use it constructively, you'll need something to write with.

You can either fill in the spaces we've left for you in these pages or you can write on your computer. You can avoid having to go back and start all over again if you realise you've not thought everything through. This can get expensive if you've brought professionals in, and it's time-consuming if you have to repeat your own work.

Of course, you can read it just to see what's in here, and come back to it when you need to get going.

If you're planning to brief someone else to build a website or a blog for you, you'll find that filling in the blanks here will help you to write a tight brief: a good set of instructions and guidelines. It will give your designers something good to work with, so they don't have to keep making changes. Changes take time and cost money, and the further along you've got, the more expensive they are going to be.

It's easier to change your web pages than reprint your paper brochure, but it still takes resources, so the more thinking and planning you do in advance, the more smoothly it will run when it comes to putting everything into place.

A FEW THINGS TO THINK ABOUT FIRST

- How much time do you have to spend on your online marketing, once this week is over and you're on your way? Do you want to build something and leave it there for a year? Will it change every day? Somewhere in between those two?
- How much money do you have? If you're going to pay someone to do the bits you don't have time or skills to do yourself, how much are you prepared to spend? What is it worth to you?
- Are you going to do it yourself? Do you want someone to do it for you? Or a mixture of the two? It's usually a question of time versus money available. Which is more important to you at the moment?
- What does your brand stand for? (And do your own people and your customers know that?)
- What do you hope to get out of your online marketing? What is its purpose?
- Who are your customers? Do you know? Is it

important? Do you want to bring in new ones? Do
you want more of the same or a different sort?

- What do you want them to do when they see your
website?

We'll be coming back to these questions, but it's a good
idea to consider them before you start. You can always
change your mind. Plans are for changing, but with no
plan at all, you can waste a lot of time.

THE BAD NEWS

Let's get this over with. There is no one straight answer,
no magic solution, no secret formula to what works and
what doesn't work online. That's why day one is spent
researching what you need to know first and day two is
the planning. It will look a lot worse for your organisation
if you do something badly, and make a half-hearted
amateurish attempt, than if you're not there at all. You've
waited this long, so do the serious thinking before you
start building anything online.

THE GOOD NEWS

Once you have the research, thinking and planning in
place, you'll build something much more useful and
interesting to your customers.

THE CREATIVE APPROACH

It's way too easy to follow a simple formula for online marketing. You register your domain name. You get someone to build your website, which says pretty much the same as everyone else's: home, our products, our people, contact us. You might start a blog, write a couple of pieces and then leave it to go out of date and be buried under new, fresh opinions online. You come up with a list of keywords when the web designers ask you to, without really thinking about what your customers look for when they search online, then you spend money on search engine optimisation without really knowing what it is for. But an agency will have done a lot of it before and you can reassure yourself that they know what they're doing. Perhaps they tempt you on to Facebook, LinkedIn and Twitter, but this seems a bit pointless when you have very few friends, links or followers taking an interest.

If you're naturally a process-based person who needs to know from the beginning exactly where each step will take you and where you'll be when you finish, follow these chapters one by one and at the end you will have a constructive, useful online presence. You'll probably need to get designers and writers in to help you when you need them.

If you're a creative type who can already imagine the result you want but don't know how to get there, resist the

The creative approach is to question absolutely everything. Why should you do any of this? How does any of this help you to achieve your purpose? Could it be done better? Could it be done differently?

temptation to rush into building something before you've done the planning. Follow the steps and you won't waste your resources building it all over again. You're more likely to want techies and a project manager to help you when you need them.

There's plenty of space in this book for you to answer the questions it will ask you. By taking a creative approach, it doesn't try to give you all the answers and fit you into a ready-made box. It asks the questions, gives you the space to come up with the answers that you need to suit your own organisation and your own customers, then gives you the tools to build a box that's the right shape and size.

THINKING AND PLANNING FOR ONLINE MARKETING

The thinking behind online marketing is the same as for any other kind of marketing, and with marketing communications the basic rule is identical: the later you make changes, the more it costs you. That's why we're starting here, rather than jumping straight into building a website on day one. If you act first and think later, you'll probably have to go back and start all over again and that will definitely be a bad use of your own time; and if you're paying someone else to do the work for you, it would be a terrible waste of your own money.

Marketing is all about balancing what you do with what customers need, now and into the future, and letting the right people know where to find it. All this, as cost effectively as possible.

When was the last time you really sat down and considered whether or not you're meeting your customers' needs? Are your competitors in a position to sneak them away from you by doing something better?

When most people talk about marketing, they are thinking of marketing communications: the things that customers see and hear about an organisation, like television and radio commercials, media coverage, websites, posters and press advertisements. They could be thinking about online social media, emails and blogs too.

Marketing communications (also called marcomms, but not by me) are all about letting your customers know what you've got for them, right now.

If you do it properly, marketing also encompasses deciding what your organisation stands for — who you are and what you do — and finding out who your customers are and how they feel about what you offer them, who your competitors are and what they are up to, planning where you want to take your organisation in the short, mid and long term, pricing strategy and building your brand identity.

Have these points covered, and your marketing communications will follow on smoothly. It's about building your foundations before you put the walls up.

Our first two chapters are on marketing foundations: research and planning. Scan them quickly if you're pretty sure that you have everything in place, to make absolutely certain that you've got everything covered. Spend more time on them if this is new to you, or if it's been a while since you gave your marketing some serious thought.

CUSTOMERS AND ORGANISATIONS

We'll be using the word "customer" to describe different kinds of people. We could be talking about:

- clients
- patients
- passengers
- supporters
- volunteers
- fans
- donors
- viewers
- delegates
- staff
- suppliers
- or someone who is in search of information, amusement or advice

They could be visiting your site for hundreds of reasons. So we'll stick to "customers" to save space. We'll use the word "organisation" for the same reason.

DAY

I

MARKETING RESEARCH

In marketing research there are three main areas to investigate:

1. Your customers
2. Your competitors
3. What big things are likely to influence your whole market

Then there's the other one that tends to take up most of your time:

4. What other interesting things are happening out there?

Before you take yourself online, it's useful to know what your customers need from you, where else they go, which sites they like, what they can't stand, if they'd like you to send them regular e-mails (or not) and whether or not they bother with social networking.

It's also essential to see what your competitors are

We do research to make sure we have the information we need to help us make the right decisions.

doing, to decide what you like about their approach and what you wouldn't touch with a barge pole.

The first question to ask yourself is: "What do I need to know?"

What issues come to mind straight away?

> *What I need to know about my customers, competitors and what's going on in my world*

If you already have an information system in place, to keep track of what your competitors are up to, what's new in your market and what your customers want from you, then you might be able to get away with only a little extra research into new developments. But if you're about to go online for the first time, it's probably worth questioning your assumptions and gathering some data that will help you give your customers what they need.

The great thing about research these days is that

you hardly need to move to find the answers to your questions. So much of it is already online. Looking online for information that already exists is called desk research, for obvious reasons. Go there first, because it's cheaper and faster than doing it yourself.

Researchers call what you get from desk research secondary data, because someone else saw it first. When you commission your own research, you get primary data. But the rule is that you only carry out your own research when you can't get the information cheaper and faster from somewhere else. This is called field research because people used to venture out "in the field" with their clipboards and observation techniques to fetch it, and still do sometimes.

Now that online research has arrived, the whole research market has changed. You can do it yourself. Like all DIY you can make mistakes, but if you're confident, give it a try. If not, there are experts you can get in to help you design a survey that will bring in the information you need.

1. YOUR CUSTOMERS

Who are they and what do they want from you? What other things do they like? What will make them want to visit your site?

(Are you sure?)

POTENTIAL PITFALL

One mistake that organisations make is to assume that they know what their customers want. In my experience, people tend to think that customers are a lot more interested in their organisation than they actually are, and that they already understand the technical terms and industry dialect that come naturally to people involved in that area of work. They don't.

Never expect customers to be experts in your own field. Start with an introduction for new visitors, and make extra information available for more knowledgeable people who want more detail.

What customers say and what customers do are often completely different things. To find out what they want you can ask them, or you can observe their behaviour.

TOP TIP

One of the brightest natural marketing researchers I ever met was a mini-cab driver who gave me a lift to the airport. He asked my advice, but he didn't need it. He was planning to invest in a minibus, but wanted to work out if his investment would pay back enough to justify the expense. He had called around all the local taxi companies and asked if they ever used minibuses. They all said yes, which was encouraging. But then he asked them all if they had any bookings for minibuses within the next week and they all said no. So he asked if they'd had any bookings for minibuses over the previous months. They still said no. He decided against buying a minibus.

This happens with huge organisations too, not just self-employed cab drivers. Where possible, don't ask what people might be intending to do; ask them what they are doing at the moment.

Customer research is all about asking the right questions.

Often companies know exactly the questions they want answered and carry out extensive research projects to find them. And yet their big project still fails. The people answering the questions very rarely lie or deliberately mislead the researcher, but often they give a picture of the way that life would be if it were perfect. That's why if you ask someone how many weeks out of the year they go to the gym, they'll probably say 52. They are not intentionally bending the truth; they are describing what they mean to do next year.

One classic error is to ask people to rate on a scale of 1 to 10 how likely they are to do something, then believe that if people put a 7 there's a 7 out of 10 chance that they will. They won't. You can only believe that they're really going to do it if they put a 10. (And even then, they might not.)

The handmade cosmetics company Lush was my main client for 14 years. In that time, they didn't commission any outside customer research, but they did value information that customers volunteered. They set up an online forum where customers were completely free to express their views, and senior staff spent time there too, including the MD, founder and head perfumer, Mark Constantine. The way they found out whether or not they were doing the right thing was to do it, and see what happened, rather than ask people what they thought they might think sometime in the future.

If you have real information available, useful sales data, e-mails and letters and feedback from customers, then use that to help you decide what to do. Then do it and see what happens. Test everything on a small scale first if you can. It's always better to try something and see what really happens than to ask people to guess what their reaction is going to be. But if you're planning a big investment, asking around first to get a general idea is safer than rushing in.

Customer research online

If you don't have enough information to help you decide what to do next, then go out and get some.

One of the ways that social media can help you get closer to your customers is to link up with them online and get a picture of who they are and what they want.

To collect your own primary data, there are some fast, simple, effective web surveys that you can use free, or pay an annual subscription to customise with your own branding and upgrade to get more features. I always use

Survey Monkey at www.surveymonkey.com for myself and for clients.

Survey Monkey is easy to use, and you can try it for nothing. If you need a way to collect data from your customers, this is an efficient, easy way to do it.

Here are some things to do, to help make your survey work better:

1. Think about what you really need to know.
2. Only ask the questions that will give you those answers.
3. Think about what you're going to do with the data when you've collected it.
4. Explain at the beginning why you're doing this, and why you need their help, and how long it's likely to take. That way, people are more likely to continue to the end.
5. Only collect data that you going to use. (If you don't need to know where they live, or how old they are, or their shoe size, don't ask. That's just nosy and it makes people feel uncomfortable.)
6. If you do need to ask personal questions, ask them at the end, not at the beginning; otherwise it sounds rude.
7. Leave plenty of space for people to give their opinions. Often the "other" box in a survey gives you far more information than the questions you thought you needed answering.

8. Before you invite your customers to take part in your survey, get your friends and family to test it for you. (Not your colleagues, they know too much about your organisation.) There are always mistakes, no matter how hard you proofread it yourself. Someone else is more likely to spot them for you.

9. Keep it as short as you can; people will get bored and leave if it's using up too much of their time.

10. Sometimes organisations offer money for filling in a survey but that can be the opposite of an incentive; paying people makes it seem like work. But a prize draw to win something small but luxurious grabs the attention.

11. Just because other surveys all seem to ask questions in a certain way doesn't mean that you have to.

12. Ask people how they feel about things to get their views.

13. Bear in mind that when people fill in questionnaires they often want to be helpful and so will err on the kindly side and be nice to you. Explain that you need to know what you and your competitors are doing wrong and ask them not to hold back.

Things to find out about my customers

Do you have the customers you want?

People who love business jargon (and I'm not one of them) talk about carrying out a gap analysis when they want to find the difference between where they are now and where they want to be. For a long time, I imagined that this was terrifically complicated, but it's not.

If the customers you have now are not the same as the kind of customers you want in future, then have a look at the gap between the two. What are the differences? Once you have identified the characteristics of your current customers and your ideal customers, you can use that to plan how to win more of the ones you want.

For example, you might want older customers because they have more spare time and money. You might want more adventurous younger customers to try out your new products. You might want larger customers with bigger budgets. Or you might want smaller customers with less bureaucracy and fewer hoops to jump through. There is no right answer, but it's good to have a clear idea of what you're aiming for.

Current customers

Ideal customers

2. YOUR COMPETITION

You know who they are. And if you don't, you ought to. How closely do you watch your competitors? How do you define who competes with you? Is it by region, by speciality, by skill? If a potential customer were looking for an organisation like yours, what would they put into a search engine to find you? And what would they come up with?

Give it a go.

Don't just use your favourite search engine. If you use Google, also try Ask Jeeves, bing or Altavista.

TOP TIP

One of my students is a very good wedding photographer. She sees her competition as other wedding photographers in the central London and Surrey area. So to find out who she is up against, she could put "wedding photographer London Surrey" into a search engine and have a very close look at who came up and what they said about themselves. She could also scrutinise the quality of their photography. For a wider picture of the general market, she could write "wedding photographer" or, more specific, "female wedding photographer".

While you're searching, make a list of the words and phrases you use in the search boxes, and see which ones get you the results closest to your own organisation. You can use these later to help bring the right people straight to your site when we come to SEO (search engine optimisation) later in the week.

Search words and phrases

Your competitors online

What do you like about their websites? What do you dislike? Do you think they are appealing to exactly the same customers? What would you do differently?

It's good business practice to see what your competitors are doing. (Although sometimes it does feel a bit sneaky.) If you feel comfortable with it, then you can subscribe to their mailing lists so you will know every time they do something new.

Spend some time researching their websites to give you an idea of where you sit in your market and how you compare to what they're doing.

How would you describe what the online design community calls the "look and feel" of their websites?

Are they classic, modern, edgy, traditional, bright, subtle, elegant, out-of-date, cutting-edge, businesslike or a bit of a mess?

What do their websites say about their organisations?

You can write down what you think here, and use it to

help you later when it comes to defining your own brand
identity online.

Competitor 1: notes

Competitor 2: notes

Competitor 3: notes

3. THE BIG STUFF

This is where we look at the big picture, the forces that influence your whole market. In marketing, it's often called a PEST analysis, which stands for political, economic, social and technological. It also gets lengthened into SLEPT, which adds "legal" to the mix, or PESTEL, which includes "environmental". Fact is, it doesn't matter. The influences on your market rarely fall into one of these carefully marked out boxes. For a start, everything is political if you choose to look at it that way.

It's easier to call it The Big Stuff, and remember to cross-reference it against any current political, economic, social, technological, legal and environmental issues that affect your business at the moment or will do in the near future.

If this is your first venture online, take a close look at what you need to stay on the right side of the law. Everything that is illegal offline is also illegal online (despite views to the contrary). Trademarks, copyright, data protection, libel... you must take care to comply online with current laws in your own country and countries in which you operate, as you would with an offline business.

All national government websites have a set of guidelines. If you're based in the UK, you can find all the information you need on the government's Department of Trade & Industry (DTI) and Department for Business Innovation & Skills (BIS) websites.

If there's an industry body that represents your market,

visit their website and put yourself on their mailing list. It's their job to keep you informed of the big stuff that will affect your organisation. Stay ahead of the game, because it can be expensive if you're found guilty of breaking the law.

In particular, make sure that you comply with the Data Protection Act 1998 and the Privacy and Electronic Communications (EC) Directive Regulations 2003 in the UK and your own country's equivalent laws. The Information Commissioner's Office (ICO) gives details of UK businesses' responsibilities and obligations to data protection.

For now, write yourself a checklist of the big influences that are influencing your industry or area of operations at the moment. Take into account all the political, economic, technological, social, environmental, and legal stuff that is affecting you at the moment.

The big stuff

4. THE INSPIRING STUFF

Take a look at current trends and fashions, and get inspiration from wherever you can find it. Watch the top ten films on YouTube. Be careful though.

> **CAUTIONARY TALE**
>
> I once sat in a big meeting when the youthful head of an online marketing department announced that he'd spent the last three days watching YouTube for "research". It's easily done, but don't announce it in a meeting if you don't want everyone to think you're a bit of a work shirker. You could easily spend all of day one - and the rest of the week - watching YouTube if you're not careful.

If you are intending to make films and put them on your site, yes you do need to see the kind of things that catch the public imagination, but an hour should do it, an evening at the most.

Find blogs (formerly known as web logs) that cover your area. Go to a search engine and write "blogs", then add words that describe the area you're interested in. That should give you a useful list to take a look at. Make a written note of good ones or add them to your bookmarks so you can go back there for inspiration.

Even from the first days of the internet, what I found astonishing was that some very smart business people had set ideas in their head about what they should produce for their own or their clients' websites, but this bore absolutely no relation to what they enjoyed doing online themselves.

CAUTIONARY TALE

Way back when I was first researching internet marketing in 1996, one very bright planning director at a major London ad agency told me all about a website that his company had been building for a luxury car client. The client had wanted to put online all the details that you could find in his cars' handbooks which would seem, these days, to be absolutely essential. But the agency had argued that this would damage the brand identity, that they had built up an image of cool sophistication and must not sully the brand by making the website appeal to the technically minded, uncool nerds who might be interested in how the engine worked. When he spoke about this, he was obviously knowledgeable and committed to his professional views, but there was no belief or passion in his voice.

Then he talked about online access at home. Smiling, and so excited he was almost bouncing up and down in his chair, he talked about how his small boy went on to the NASA site and looked up lots of details about space rockets. What stood out for me was that he was unable to apply his personal experience of the internet to help his clients create an interesting, useful site for their customers.

True, it was 1996, but nothing has changed. People still allow their websites to be built for them with no passion or excitement for what's on there.

That's why this section of your research should be

about your own interests. Which websites do you think are absolutely brilliant? Why? What's great about them? What can you borrow from them for your own website? Even if it's on a smaller scale. And if you've already delved that far into the information superhighway, explain why you choose to follow your favourite blogs. Which friends' and organisations' Facebook statuses and tweets do you enjoy reading? Why is that?

Here are some examples from people whose opinions I value. It's not enough just to name the sites you like; you need to interrogate yourself until you come up with an answer to the question, "What is it that makes this site so good?"

Claire Carroll, actor:
- Amazon: "It's simple and user-friendly."
  www.amazon.com / www.amazon.co.uk

Lucie Gray, designer:
"It's little people like me having a say, honesty, no business jargon or marketing rubbish."
- Design Sponge: "Inspiring stuff!"
  www.designspongeonline.com
- Noisy Decent Graphics, Ben Terrett's blog: "Mixing the love for design and marketing, gives the feeling that he knows what he's doing and can be trusted to do a good job because he's passionate."
  http://noisydecentgraphics.typepad.com

- Swiss Miss, Swiss designer in New York, her blog: "Fab blog, interesting stuff and a great way for a small company to advertise. Wish I had the time!" www.swiss-miss.com

Tony Rowlands, accountant:
- HM Revenue & Customs: "Huge tax information content — professionally indispensible." www.hmce.gov.uk
- The Big Project, a portal with links to top sites in different popular categories; not pretty, but useful: "Online news from everywhere, anytime." www.thebigproject.co.uk
- Multimap: "Instant directions and locations." www.multimap.com

Ally Hill, yoga teacher:
- Amazon: "Easy to find what you want and you can see/hear samples."
- Joe Browns, clothing and accessories: "Easy to navigate." www.JoeBrowns.co.uk.
- YogaMatters, yoga supplies, books and music: "Simple design." www.yogamatters.co.uk

Sarah McCartney, counsellor (This is not me; it's my friend. I found her when I Googled myself. Long story.):

- Ocado, online supermarket: "Reliable; easy search engine." www.ocado.com
- Bravissimo, lingerie shop, integrating online shopping with live customer service: "Easy to use, if I need to talk to someone, I can phone up and a member of staff will discuss the products with me as if I were in the shop. Very friendly staff, do not seem rushed. I always end up spending more because they are so helpful." www.bravissimo.com

Emma Runciman, researcher:

- Amazon: "(Sorry for the slightly dull choice, but I do love it.) So easy to use. The suggestions and 'more items to consider' are usually spot-on."
- Shopworks: "The second I land on this website I know exactly what they do. They've even managed to neatly drop in testimonials on most pages; these make me want to find out more. This company looks credible and trustworthy straight away." www.shopworks.co.uk
- Dirt Mountain Bike Magazine: "It's simple and is updated very regularly. Only need to look at one column to see updates. Great community feel, comments and contributions welcome." http://dirtmag.co.uk

Anna Penrose, email marketer:

- Facebook: "It's constantly updated and intuitive... although it does have its faults." www.facebook.com
- The Eden Project: "It is so beautiful and updated with new content and images regularly. I don't really have any reason to use it; I just think it is gorgeous, especially at Christmas."
- Amazon: "It's honest, transparent and easy to use."

Pete Cornes, writer:

- Slashdot, news for nerds: "It's not cool, and it's not pretty. But it's standards-compliant and fantastically usable. The personality's strong (but geeky), which comes through from the little touches. And it developed as a hybrid between a BBS and a proto-social network, and it got the community thing right from the start. http://slashdot.org
- La Fraise, amazing t-shirt design competition and shop: "Community driven. Intuitive navigation. Cute design." www.lafraise.com

Roger Horberry, copywriter:

- Visual blogs www.ffffound.com and www.thisisnthappiness.com: "Inspiration, entertainment and keeping up with the visual zeitgeist."

- Wikipedia: "Accessible and an idea I believe in."
www.wikipedia.com

Hossay Momand, cosmetics manufacturer:
- ASOS (as seen on screen), clothing and accessories
retailer: "Great multi-delivery options, which are
clearly shown on the site, easy navigation, zoom-
in features on products, and short videos where
required." www.asos.com
- Apotcare, cosmetics: "Visuals, graphics, plenty of
information but not overloaded."
www.apotcare.oxatis.com

You might notice that nobody mentioned that they
like to see flashy graphics on a website or were impressed
by complexity. Yet, for some reason, when people building
or commissioning websites decide what it is that they
want, they get really excited about introducing amazing
new features. Think about featuring what your customers
really want, not everything that's possible.

You probably also noticed how many recommendations
Amazon got. If you haven't been there for a while, go back
and spend some time and money to see why it's rated
so highly: good value, useful, interesting, entertaining,
interactive, helpful. It ticks all the boxes.

Revisit some of your favourite sites and make a note
here of what it is that appeals to you:

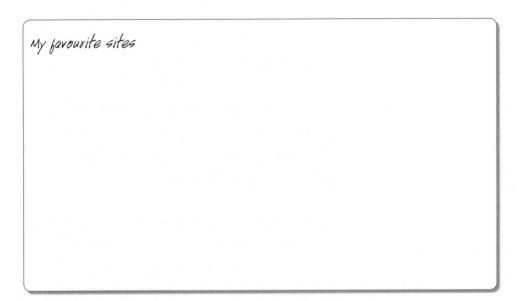

My favourite sites

P.S. THE UNINSPIRING STUFF

What annoys you when you go online? Here's a list of irritating features named by my helpful contributors. Aim to avoid them.

"Flash images which take forever to load and poor navigation tools." — Ally Hill

"Really shonky usability. Unintuitive navigation. Features thrown in for the hell of it. And — of course — bad writing." — Pete Cornes

"Too many buttons so you can't find what you're looking for quickly." — Lucie Gray

"Pop-ups. And then pop-ups. Flashing lights and excessive colour." — Tony Rowlands

"Far too much information, lack of attention to navigation and the auto scroll box that forces you to sign up and won't shift until an email address is entered." — Hossay Momand

"Difficulty with navigating around site, not clearly marked; I hate having to register before I get any info — it's like an over-persistent salesperson in a shop — I run out of the shop if I just want to browse and they keep asking if they can help. If websites ask for me to register just to look at something or buy something, I want to sign off." — Sarah Pierce

"Too much on the front page." — Sarah McCartney

"Flash intros — thankfully these seem to be disappearing. Sites where graphic design appears to be more important than usability and functionality. A site needs to work as well as look great. Both can be achieved." — Emma Runciman

"Poorly spelt, bad grammar, infantalisation of the user, unoriginality, too much going on or too complicated to use." — Rick Senley

"The usual suspects — poor usability, poor copy, prioritisation of design/programming bells and whistles over function, too much of everything."
— Roger Horberry

DAY
2

PLANNING

It's really tempting to leap straight in with both feet and start tweeting on Twitter, or writing your views on a blog. Before you do that, decide what you want to achieve and how you want to present yourself. This chapter is here to guide you through the thinking, so you'll save time later on when it comes to the doing.

I. YOUR PURPOSE

Your objectives for being online will influence your online strategy. Do you want:

- To be talked about
- To bring in more clients
- To change the kinds of clients you attract
- To build your brand identity
- To sell your products with an online shop
- To take bookings
- To reassure people that they've made the right decision
- To be influential

"... I've noticed the tech side is sometimes a barrier to thinking about the strategy, the bit you really need to think about." — Emma Runciman

- To demonstrate your skills
- To provide information
- To ask for donations
- A combination of those things
- Something different?

Every organisation and individual has a different reason for going online. Decide your purpose before you start and you won't waste resources on elements that you don't need.

Here are three completely different opinions from small, independent businesses. Perhaps they'll ring a few bells with you, or you might disagree completely. They are here to help you consider what you need.

a. Emma Runciman, Researcher, Think.Say.Do.

"My online marketing efforts have really boosted my brand. I don't see my online brand identity as separate, I see it as complimentary. I go to networking events, then encourage people to look at my online presence. If I first make contact with people online, I encourage them to meet me or speak on the phone."

b. Roger Horberry, Copywriter

"Think of it as a delivery mechanism for your portfolio and CV — nothing more. Don't get me wrong — I like and need my site, but it's a very minor part of the mix. Anyone in my line of work who is attracting lots of new business through their online efforts is clearly doing something I ain't. I'd be very interested to hear how they do it (if indeed they genuinely do do it).

"No-one buys my services cos I've cobbled together a halfway decent site; they buy because they have a specific problem they want me to make go away. All my effective marketing is face-to-face or word of mouth."

c. Anna Penrose, Email Marketer, MailAway

"What's been brilliant was creating a blog. It's helped with generating a reputation for me personally and creating a brand for my business. I can't rant enough about how many benefits I think there are to a company blog. To name a few: keep in touch with customers, improve SEO, duplicate content for email newsletters and other social media sites (like SlideShare or YouTube). It is also very encouraging when you meet someone who says, 'I just love your blog. Can you give me some advice?'"

Anna uses her blog to bring in new business, Roger uses his website purely as an online CV and Emma combines the two.

Stick with your purpose, whether you are building your own site or getting experts in to do it for you.

The point is that everyone has a different reason for being online. Work out what you want to achieve before you do anything. Then you'll have something to measure against to help you check that you're doing the right thing.

Think about why you want people to visit your website and what you want them to do when they get there. Here's a space to write about it:

What I want from being online

"Get a strategy. Think about what you want to do and work out what's the best way to do it."
— Pete Cornes, www.pilcrow.co.uk

II. YOUR STRATEGY
How can you achieve your purpose?

Your strategy is what you do to help you to achieve your purpose, to get where you want to be.

Your purpose is your reason for being there in the first place. Often people forget about their purpose, and get bogged down in the day-to-day details, the operational side. To keep the excitement and the energy flowing through your organisation, you have to remind yourself why you started along this route.

> *What is my organisation's purpose?*

A marketing strategy is typically made up of five to seven ways of working that all help to take you there.

It's handy to have a strategy in place to remind you to spend time on things that will help you to achieve your purpose and objectives and not to waste time on things that won't.

Here's a general-purpose strategy that would do nicely for the kind of business organisations I typically work with:

Purpose: To help organisations to communicate better with their customers and their staff

Objective: Annual turnover of £250,000, growing to £1,000,000 in five years

Online Marketing Strategy:

- Update our website and blog regularly to show new and current clients examples of our work, with testimonials to reassure visitors that we are doing a good job.
- Keep the trade informed and interested in what we're doing.
- Offer an online training service for distance learning.
- Send monthly emails to current, past and potential clients.

- Register on free directories.
- Implement low-cost SEO.
- Expand our online network by using social media.

Advertising online — yes or no?

If a web consultant says that you absolutely must buy online advertising or you'll lose out, you can ask how exactly it will help to achieve your purpose. If it does, great, but if it doesn't, then use your resources on something that will.

Organisations which work on personal recommendation need websites that are reassuring, that give potential customers the information they need to be certain they are making the right decision investing their own time and money with that organisation. Their design, text, look and feel should be precisely consistent with their real-world brand identity. But there's no need to use additional funds for online ads when it would be better spent on going to conferences and meeting new people, and sending email newsletters to current and previous happy clients.

But then again, businesses which sell their products online to customers around the world need an efficient online shop with a constant supply of new customers. Using advertising to bring in new customers could be vital in making the business successful.

Blogging

If you are operating in an area where changes happen fast,

and you need to give regular updates, then you might want to write a blog, to keep your customers interested and informed. Blogs are useful for people in the creative industry too when they can post new photographs, illustrations, press appearances and articles in a few minutes to remind their customers what they're up to.

Your online marketing strategy should work with your real-world approach. We'll come back to this on Day Six after you've had a chance to think about your options, and what's best for you and your organisation. For the moment, here's a space for ideas.

How might I use online marketing to achieve my organisation's purpose?

Who do you want your customers to be?

How does your ideal customer compare with the customers you have now? What would you like them to think about you?

All through this book, you'll be reminded to consider your customers; if you only concentrate on what it is you do, and see everything from your own point of view, they might get bored and find somewhere else to

The single most important thing to remember is to see everything you do from your customers' point of view. If you forget that, then you'll lose them.

go online where they feel that their needs are being taken into account, somewhere they feel welcome and more comfortable. That's obviously true when you see them face-to-face, but it's even more true online where they can walk away without you ever knowing.

People feel a surprising loyalty to online businesses and web resources where they find something useful to them. A computer screen is not a barrier; it's an open door. See it that way, invite visitors in, make them feel comfortable and they'll be back.

On Day One, we were thinking about what you already know about your current customers and how they're different from the kind you want in future. What are their good points? What makes a great customer? What makes an ideal customer? How can you find more of those?

A creative approach to considering your customers
This might look a bit like we're kidding around, but it's serious. Ad agencies do this stuff and charge thousands for it. The reason they do it is because it helps to get inside the minds of the people you are talking to and to imagine what they're thinking at the same time as you're trying to get their attention. It doesn't matter if you can't draw; do it anyway.

Imagine the kind of customer you'd like to have more of and describe them. Here are a couple I made up to give you an idea.

Name: Alex

Age: 43

What he does: Alex runs the customer services department of a chain of organic food shops in the UK that has just ventured overseas. They have two shops in Dubai and three in Paris.

What he did yesterday: He got up at 7.30 a.m., showered, grabbed a yoghurt for breakfast and didn't have much time to say goodbye to the kids and his partner. He was in the office at 8.40 a.m., and dealt with e-mails from Dubai before he went into a 9.15 a.m. meeting with his UK managers. For the rest of the day, he seemed to be running around and trying to respond to questions he'd already told everyone the answers to. He dealt with three irritated customers who had not got the results they needed from his staff or their managers. The phone only stopped ringing when he went into meetings and turned it off.

He's worried that his staff turnover rate is too high, that his people don't know enough to answer his customers' questions and he's having to do their job too. He believes that the customer is always right, but he's a bit tired of having to agree with them and admitting his company's mistakes. He got home at 8 p.m., in time to put his tired-out boy to bed. His little girl was already fast asleep. He went to bed worrying what to do with his life, and if all this is worth it just to have a nice house in two weeks in France every summer.

When he visits my website: He's hoping to find someone who can come in and revolutionise online communication between his staff and his customers, so they can find out things themselves without having to call him over every tiny detail. He wants to feel reassured, relieved, excited and adventurous.

I'd like him to: Pick up the phone.

Name: Lynette

Age: 33

What she does: Lynette has started up her own knitwear design business. She has an online shop and sells her clothes at the designer market in her city's development district. Hers is a social enterprise. She employs knitters who have had difficulty finding work and pays them fairly. As a result, her prices are higher than those of fashion shops. She relies on her amazing designs to bring in the business.

What she did yesterday: She picked up 10 spectacular finished coats from her local knitting team, received a delivery of 10 big boxes of Italian cotton yarn and was kindly given another five boxes of spare wool from a Scottish mill, so now she can scarcely move in her office. She called two fashion editors about featuring the coats; one was interested, maybe. She was up until midnight finishing the patterns and instructions for the spring collection of cardigans to send out to her knitters. And her mother has come to stay.

When she visits my website: She's looking for someone to write weekly updates for her blog and to write press releases for her. I want Lynette to feel relieved, confident and keen to get in touch.

I'd like her to: Join my mailing list, at the very least, and email. I would like her to read from start to finish, but she probably doesn't have the time, so I'd like her to read enough to be reassured that she's come to the right place.

These people aren't real. They aren't even close to genuine clients. I just made them up. But they are the kind of people that I do and would like to work with, and it helps me to consider their real lives and the things they have on their minds when I'd like to think that I have their full attention.

Make up a couple of clients of your own. The more realistic a life you give them, the easier it will be for you to see your organisation from an outsider's point of view.

Name:

Age:

What he does:

What he did yesterday:

When he visits my website:

I'd like him to:

Name:

Age:

What she does:

What she did yesterday:

When she visits my website:

I'd like her to:

III. YOUR ORGANISATION

First, write down in a few sentences what it is that your organisation does. How would you explain this simply to someone new?

Who we are and what we do

You can come back to this if you need to; it's what people sometimes call their "elevator pitch", the idea that they can tell someone what they do in 30 seconds, the time that an elevator takes to reach your floor. It's an American term. (Europeans don't usually have that long because the lift doesn't go up so many floors, but you get the general idea.)

You must be able to explain it clearly and quickly so that the people you are telling can decide if they want to hear more. If you can't do it in less than a couple of minutes, they might lose the will to live while you're talking. They'll certainly lose the will to listen.

When you're online, look at some organisations that you deal with and see what they say about themselves.

While you're here, have a look at these:

PETE CORNES, WRITER:

"I love boring writing.

"It's what I get up for in the morning. Seriously. The duller and more leaden, the better.

"Why? Because if business waffle didn't exist, no-one would ever notice sparkling, compelling writing.

"But corporate claptrap's here to stay. Which means the right words can make a real difference. The difference between your customers listening in or tuning out.

"And if you want to get the words right, you need a professional writer. Someone whose linguistic radar's accurate enough to pick out what's working and what's not.

"So can I suggest someone?

"Me."

CLAIRE CARROLL, ACTOR, ABOUT BEEF ENCOUNTER:

"A show with one woman and a lot of cows...

"Written and performed by Claire Carroll, Beef Encounter is a one-woman show which tells the story of reluctant rambler and renowned food critic Belinda Donovan, who gets separated from her group on a walking holiday. Confronted by a herd of cows, her fast talking takes her from fear and loathing to quite another level. Can bovine be best for Belinda in her journey of discovery and self-realisation? Will she run with the herd, or from the herd? In just 45 funny and poignant minutes in the company of cows, Belinda learns more about herself than she has in the last 45 years."

RICK SENLEY, PHOTOGRAPHER:

"English photographer and journalist Rick Senley, shortlisted in 2008 for Travel Photographer of the Year, takes pictures that reflect his passion for travel and people. His work ranges from portraits of villains, boxers, soldiers and musicians to documenting celebrity parties and travelling gypsies. Rick has worked for companies such as Sony Ericsson, AA Travel Guides and Coutts Banks and is regularly used by charities such as Unicef and the National Deaf Children's Society, for whom he photographed a cross-India bike ride."

MERCHANTS OF VINO:

"Welcome to Merchants of Vino.

"As Robert Louis Stephenson so rightly said, 'Wine is bottled poetry.'

"Merchants of Vino is the brainchild of Debra Smith-Symmonds, Sarah Peirce and Louise Heasman.

"Our philosophy is that wine should be enjoyed. Learning about wine and discovering new tastes should be fun. We all have our personal favourites, and there is no right or wrong taste, but by trying different wines, and being introduced to some new exciting wine producers, we are going on a journey of discovery."

PRINTHOUSE, PRINTERS:

"We're a good London printer with a unique history.

"Back in 1990, our young founder started us up during the days when design and print was just emerging from the dark ages. His vision: to create a great London printer.

"Over the years, PrintHouse has grown by being techno geeks, embracing the latest design, pre-press and print technology. We love our toys because we can print faster, better and cheaper for you! Best of all, we're a London printer on your doorstep.

"Nearly two decades on, our Park Royal, London, NW10, operation has some great kit, including two flagship monster B1 Heidelberg presses. Next to these giants, we operate smaller Heidelbergs and a variety of digital small and large format machines. So if it's ink on paper that you need - we have a solution ready to rock and roll.

"Oh, and that founder of ours, he left us and went off to work elsewhere — as a Member of Parliament!"

MAILAWAY:

"Email marketing has never been so simple.

"Keeping in touch with your contacts has just become a whole lot easier. MailAway helps you to send beautiful email campaigns, track the results and manage your subscribers. It really is email marketing made simple."

When it comes to describing your own organisation, you might choose to write the final version yourself or decide to get a professional copywriter in. It depends on your own skills and what you enjoy doing, balanced with how much money you have in the kitty. For the moment, give it your best shot. Think how you'd describe your organisation to the ideal customers that you wrote about earlier in the chapter. Here's a space for notes.

How I'd describe my organisation

IV. YOUR BRAND

Every organisation has a brand identity, even if it hasn't invested time working on it. It's crucial that you stop and think about yours. Considering what your customers think of your brand is essential too. If the way you see your organisation is different from the way your customers see your organisation, then you need to put some serious work into bridging the gap.

These days, a brand is not just a logo. It's everything that influences the impression you give to your customers. Whenever you start to think about marketing communications, online or in the real world, you've got to be conscious of your brand identity.

POTENTIAL PITFALL

Some small businesses, self-employed people and campaigning organisations have told me (perhaps a little defensively): "I don't have a brand and I don't need one." That is to misunderstand what branding is all about. Brands are great tools to help you make your communication clear. It helps to distinguish you from others like you and to make what you do more memorable. When we talk about branding, it's much more than sticking a logo on something so that you can charge more for it. It's about giving yourself a recognisable, consistent identity that people feel they can rely on.

If you're heading online for the first time, now is a good opportunity to think about your branding and what your organisation stands for: your brand values.

CAUTIONARY TALE: CONSIGNIA

In the world of marketing, it's not uncommon to see a new marketing director or head of branding come in and decide to change everything. There are big salaries and they need to justify their existence. Sometimes it needs changing; often it doesn't. It might just need a small tweak — slight sharpening of the logo, minor alteration of the colour, modernisation of the typeface. If you have a recognisable brand that customers like, then don't mess with it. The Post Office changed to Consignia and back again so quickly that almost everyone has managed to blot it from their memories. What on earth were they thinking? (And I'm not implying that the Consignia team did it to justify their existence. I'm sure they thought it was a good idea at the time. It just wasn't.)

Other idiotic rebranding includes renaming college libraries "Learning Resource Centres". Don't do it for the sake of it, and don't chuck the baby out with the bathwater.

There are some excellent rebrands and new brands. For ideas, look at some of the top design agencies, like Pentagram and Elmwood, for inspiration. If you're thinking about bringing a designer in to help you with your visual brand indentity — and this is a very good idea — do your thinking and planning, and have your brand values in place ready for your first meeting. Then they'll be much more likely to come back with something that suits you, in a lot less time.

Brand values are the most important part of branding, far more important than your logo, your font or your strapline. Your values are your foundation. Thinking about your purpose, make a list of your organisation's values. If your organisation is just made up of you and your skills, it's no different from a multinational employing thousands of people. Just smaller and easier to control.

Here are some examples of organisations' brand values:
- reliable, traditional, family-run, polite
- experimental, unusual, dynamic
- ethical, sustainable, spiritual, welcoming
- cheap, cheerful, no-frills, chatty
- international, technological, cutting-edge, powerful
- challenging, innovative, urban, modern

- campaigning, dedicated, purposeful, focused
- friendly, enthusiastic, creative, groundbreaking

Our brand values

Once you define your brand values, you can use them to help you decide how to behave towards customers so that everything you do reinforces this. Your designs and your writing should reflect them. Pin them down, and all your marketing becomes simpler.

The images and words you use for your online marketing should all help to build your brand. Use your brand values as a basis for deciding what to choose and your brand will become more recognisable. The same applies to your use of colour, the typefaces that you choose and the style of your design.

There are some creative exercises which people in the world of branding have done for years to help them through their thinking. Again, this might look a little too trivial to be businesslike, but once you've tried you'll see that it's an excellent creative technique for helping you to think clearly.

THE BISCUIT ANALYSIS

If your brand was a biscuit, what kind of biscuit would it be?

What makes you think that?

What kind of biscuit would your customers choose to represent your brand?

How would you explain that?

If there is a difference, why do you think that is?

Which biscuit would you like your brand to be?

How would you describe that biscuit?

The Brief

In advertising and marketing, a brief is a set of guidelines and instructions that you give to a creative team, designer, copywriter, photographer and anyone else who is going to go away and use their imaginations to make something happen for you. The better the brief, the more likely they are to come back with something very close to what you want. If you tell them to go away and do whatever they like and give them complete freedom without telling them anything about your organisation and where you want to take it, you can waste an awful lot of time (and money). All good creative people work better when they're given a well defined brief.

Even if you're going to do all the creative work yourself, it's always best to write the brief first. It will help you to stay focused on getting where you need to be.

Your online marketing brief can include all of the

following, and anything else you want to add that you think will be helpful:

- purpose
- objectives, this year and into the future
- online strategy
- who your customers are and what they want
- brand values
- budget and timing
- the look and feel of your design
- creative styles you already use for your brand (typefaces, colours, tone of voice)

The brief

Now you have an idea of what you stand for, what you need to say, who you want to say it to, and what you want them to do when they've seen what you're all about. So you're ready to put it into practice.

DAY
3

GETTING STARTED WITH
WEBSITES AND BLOGS

You'll need a computer with an internet connection, and the brief you wrote at the end of the last chapter. If you've got a logo and a photograph of yourself, they'll come in handy too.

This is your practice run to test out what's there, find out how simple it is, check what you like doing and what you're good at, and what it's best to leave to the experts.

Here are some reasons people give me for not getting started:

- It's too complicated for me to do myself.
- I don't have the design skills.
- It's going to cost a fortune for someone else to build.
- It's going to cost even more to update.

You can forget about all that.

You don't *have* to have your own website or blog. You can get by with the intelligent use of social media. You can carry out all your online marketing with a Facebook profile and your own page, Twitter and emails. But it's so simple these days, you might as well get on with it.

One concern about starting out with your own web presence is that it might cost you a fortune. Of course some websites cost millions to build and run, but you're not Amazon yet and you can have a small site up and running for a few days' business income, maybe a month's worth if you want something special.

But you can build a website or start a blog for nothing. Or you can pay a little to have a few more features. These days, building a website from a template is so ridiculously easy that you'll kick yourself for not having tried it sooner.

You can't always do exactly what you want with a simple template; for that, you'll need to learn some programming skills like HTML and CSS, or bring in a designer. See what you can do yourself, then decide if you hit a technological barrier. What you can do is to build a site that looks very passably professional. Stick to your brand values, and keep asking yourself what it is that your customers need to know and follow the intuitive, step-by-step instructions on screen.

There are so many different sites you can use to build and host your own website or blog — and they are redesigned so regularly to make them even easier — that there is no point printing pictures of computer screens in this book and telling you which buttons to press. The best way to learn is to get on with it.

WEBSITE, BLOG OR BOTH?

If all you need is a small site with basic information about who you are, what you do and how to get in touch, then you can start to build it today and probably finish it too. If you spent Day One looking at different websites and blogs, then you probably have an idea of which will suit you best.

On a simple website, you can show the information your customers need under several different headings. They'll be able to click on different buttons or tabs to get around and find out everything they need about you in minutes. If you aren't going to update your site on a regular basis, stick to a website because blogs are supposed to be updated regularly, and it always looks a bit shabby to click on one to find out what's new and discover that nothing's happened in the last six months. That would give your visitors a bad impression.

A blog is more like an online diary which everyone can read. If your organisation is all about what's new and gives out regular updates, then blogging will suit you best.

You can also build a website which has a blog section, getting the best of both worlds. At the time of writing, my favourite designers are all using WordPress to create customised sites with blogs included.

DIY OR PS?

Are you going to do it yourself, or pay someone?

Unless you plan to build a business designing websites for other organisations, or you particularly enjoy it, there's no need to spend time learning web design skills.

You can get an expert in to construct your site so it does exactly what you need, and a designer to make it look perfect on every different kind of browser that your customers could possibly be using: old, new, popular or obscure. They'll make it work well, look good and show up on search engines, and you won't have to spend time learning to do it yourself. It'll also leave you free to get on with running your own organisation, rather than spending time on DIY.

The advantages of DIY are that it's free, fast (once you've got the hang of it) and you have control.

The advantage if you're buying someone's skills and experience to personalise your site to your exact specifications is that it'll probably look a lot better than anything you can manage yourself.

WHAT ARE YOU GOING TO CALL IT?

If you already run an organisation, you'll want a name that is the same, or as close as possible to the one you already use so that people can find you easily. With a blog, you don't have to register and pay for a domain name but if you want your organisation to look businesslike online, it's good to have your own domain name or URL (unique resource locator) like a .com or .co.uk or .eu.

When the web started up, people bought up domain names such as www.harrods.com cheaply and waited until the brand owners caught up with them, then asked for a lot of money to release them. Now, intellectual property law has caught up with them; sitting on a domain name that is nothing to do with your organisation is counted as "passing off" — pretending to be something you're not — so you have to be able to prove that you can represent the organisation whose domain name you are buying.

To see if your domain name is free, visit a website that sells them and put your name into the search box. Put "domain names" into a search engine and it will come up with a list of companies that will find what's available, and register it for you, for a small price. It's worth checking, but generally a .com is the most expensive (but still only around £20) and regional ones are cheaper (from around £2.99 at the moment).

Websites that do this include:

- www.create.net
- www.1and1.com or .co.uk
- www.discountdomains.co.uk
- www.buydomains.com

Put your company name in the search box, tick the click box for the region or category you want, like .eu or

.me.uk or .info, then click to see if it's available. If someone already has it, then you'll be given some alternatives. You can buy up several of them and point them all at the same site. For example, Selfridges' store is online at selfridges.com, but if you type in selfridges.co.uk, it sends you straight to the .com site.

FREE WEBSITES

- www.wix.com: My nephew built his website www.guitarlute.co.uk for his lute and guitar restoration business on Wix.
- www.weebly.com: Claire Carroll built www.beefencounter.com for her one-woman show on Weebly.

Go to either of these, or search online for "free websites" and visit the different options.

Free sites are free for a reason; they don't have many features and they will keep on contacting you to nudge you into upgrading, but if you're happy with the strings attached, then go ahead and take advantage. It's a good way to practise.

GOOD-VALUE WEBSITES

My favourite is www.create.net, but feel free to choose your own. I like basekit.com too. Once you've subscribed to Create or whichever you choose, you'll be guided gently through the set-up, and you'll have access to masses of advice on how to improve your site and market it online. You build it online, and they host your site for you, so you pay a monthly charge for that. There are loads of bolt-on extra features to use: you have the option to add a blog, a shop and links to your profiles on the social networking sites you use, and more.

FREE BLOGS

Blogs are best for a constant flow of new stuff; that's why so many fashion companies and trend-spotters use them. They're good for journalists, photographers, shops and anyone who wants to say, "Look what just happened." They're great for comments on life in general. Yes, they are also used by teenagers to give you the latest updates on their lives, but no-one's making you read blogs you don't want to.

Go to one of these and give it a go, or find more options using a search engine:

- www.wordpress.org
- www.typepad.com
- www.blogger.com
- www.blog.co.uk
- www.tumblr.com

BALANCING TIME AND MONEY

At what point do you bring someone in to do the job

for you? When you run out of time and it becomes more valuable than your money. That's the point at which you pay someone who's got the skills and experience to do a better job of it than you, in a lot less time.

If you are fast and efficient at working on a computer, it'll only take you a day to set up your own site with all the functions you need, so go ahead and do it yourself. If you don't have the budget yet to pay someone, then you've got to get on with it and like it. The central path is to bring in someone who does this kind of thing for a hobby and who'll work for less money, but you do have to keep an eye on them and make sure that they stick to the brief.

You might reach a point where you want to do something more complicated than a simple template will allow, so pay someone to do it for you. On the other hand, you might spend the rest of your working life happily tinkering with your site and updating it when you need to without ever paying more than a small hosting fee. You don't know until you try it.

There will always be predatory businesses around who will take your money and run. But most website builders, writers and designers want to work with you and keep your business over the long term, so they want to be good value and reliable. They work on personal recommendation, like most of us do. Ask people you know. You can also visit websites that you like the look of, scroll down to the bottom, find the small print and see who built them.

BASIC DESIGN

For masses of good ideas, go to the brilliant Inspiration Hut www.inspirationhut.net, run by Abbie May Davey and Tom White, design and photography students from Plymouth College.

A short note on using colour

If you already have a logo, colours that you always use and a regular group of typefaces, stick with them. That way, your customers will feel that they've arrived at the right place.

Keep the background light and use colour sparingly. Selfridges use their bright yellow all over their carrier bags to make them stand out in a London street, but when you visit their website, the background is plain white with yellow features every now and again. You don't want your customers to feel ill looking at it.

Remind yourself of your brand values. What first impression do you want your visitors to get? See everything from your customers' point of view, and if you find yourself getting too close to your own project to put some perspective on it, ask someone you know whose opinion you value to be honest with you about what you've done.

You have to decide for yourself whether or not you want to bring in professionals to help you with your project, and you won't know until you try, but here are some views from owners and small organisations who are online themselves.

"Get someone to manage some elements for you, or it's very time-consuming. It's a pain in the butt trying to set up a website yourself, especially if you have an online shop." — Sarah Pierce, www. merchantsofvino.com

"Find a website designer you get on with and understand." — Rick Senley, www.ricksenley.com

"Social network interaction you can do yourself. Website copy needs to be done by a professional copy writer who knows what should and shouldn't be said and how to properly convey it in a short snappy sentence." — Hossay Momand, www.yllume.com

"Depends how techy you are. It's very useful to be able to tweak your site yourself, so some basic HTML might be useful." — Roger Horberry, www. rogerhorberry.com

"Depends on your technical appetite. I've got professional graphic design and done all my own CSS, a personal theme, hooks in the code etc etc. Most people wouldn't. At the very least, get the visual design done by someone who gets it." — Pete Cornes, www.pilcrow.co.uk

"A blog template and a designer will do for many. You can learn first and then do a second version with more cash. Get experts for designing and coding of site, but you should write the brief." — Anon.

"Get an expert to help with the tech side — setting up blogs on sites, producing an email template." — Emma Runciman, http://thinksaydo.co.uk

"I would say that small businesses need to do as much as possible themselves at first and not commit to large costs. My husband, Dave, designed my website, then read about SEO and did that too." — Sarah McCartney, www.symmetrycounselling.co.uk

"If you can't do the website yourself, find someone who can, but be sure you know what you want. A web designer is only as good as their brief. You can easily do a newsletter yourself and e-mail that out to interested parties as well as posting it on your website." — Ally Hill, www.sarva.co.uk

"Pay for website design. Do most other things yourself." — Tony Rowlands, www.ajrowlands.com

"Get a graphic designer on board. Image is everything!" — Lucie Gray, graphic designer, www.facebook.com/lucie.gray

Honestly, once you get going there, you'll wonder why on earth you were worrying about it. In the words of Nike, just do it. Don't publish it just yet, though.

CAUTIONARY TALE: PUBLISHING TOO EARLY
It is so simple to create your own website using a template, that you might be tempted to rush in and get started, then publish it before you're quite sure it's finished. You can always go back in there and change things — that's the great thing about doing your own — but always check the whole site with the "preview" tool before you rush to get it online.

One of my students showed me her friend's website. She had finished the home page and pressed the button to publish it to the web, where the whole world could see it. But she had forgotten to tick the boxes which stop all the other pages showing up too. So when anyone clicked the tab that said "About Us", it showed an empty space saying, "This is where you can upload a photo if you like," and where the text ought to have been, it said, "Here's where you write something about yourself." Apart from giving them a good laugh, this also gives customers the impression that you are impulsive and don't check details. Not a great way to run a business.

Get some of your friends and colleagues — and customers if they're willing — to check the site before you publish it; they will spot things that you've missed.

Next, what to put in it.

DAY
4

CREATIVE WORK
(ALSO KNOWN AS "CONTENT")

So what are you going to put on your website, your blog, your Facebook page and everything else you choose to do online to let people know what your organisation is up to? In the online industry, people use the word "content" when they mean all the words and pictures you're going to use to communicate your purpose and your brand values.

Write down your brand values here to remind you what you are aiming at.

"Make it easy to use. Get people involved. Show your personality. And always keep an eye on what you're trying to do, not how you're doing it."
— Pete Cornes

My brand values

CAUTIONARY TALE

Another student of mine, a tech-savvy chap who runs an IT security business, told me on day one of the course all about the proposal for his company's website. He said that he'd already briefed it in and then closed his laptop and folded his arms and sat back smiling. All done; there was nothing I could teach him. Who was writing the text for it? He sat up again.

"Content! I'd forgotten about that," he said.

Many people in the creative industries loathe the word content for web creative work (including me). It implies that someone else has done the important part, building the structure, and now all we have to do is to fill up the available space with random stuff. Instead of starting with a structure, then wondering how to fill it, it's a good idea to think about the structure, words, pictures and design all at the same time to make them work together better.

DECIDING BETWEEN DIY AND PS

If you are a good photographer or illustrator, then go ahead and try out your own creative work, but if you can afford a professional, use them. They can make a basic website look magnificent. You can also make a well-constructed, beautifully designed website look like a dog's dinner by using third-rate creative work.

Play to your strengths. If you've got the talents, use them. If you don't, and you do have a budget, think seriously about bringing people in to do the creative work for you. Give them a good brief so you get the best value and top quality work quickly, without having to go back and forth making changes.

FILLING IN THE BLANKS

Now that you've experimented with structure, let's consider the creative work you'll be using, and match them up to create a good online presence, which is:

- interesting
- useful
- entertaining
- valuable
- amusing
- preferably a combination of at least two of those things

POTENTIAL PITFALL: MOVING IMAGES

I got an email recently about some web software that I could use to make all the graphics move on my website. "Affordable, new, exciting!" it said. Would you buy it and add moving graphics just because you can? Are you sure you'd want to do that? When you see a website with moving bits and pieces, do you find it interesting or does it drive you round the bend?

Human perception is arranged to allocate more attention to things that move than things that sit still. That's why we can look out over a whole landscape and our attention is drawn to a bird several streets away. When we evolved, things that moved were either edible or could harm us. So now, we can't turn this brain function off. That's why web developers use moving things to attract a response. But do think carefully about using them; they can be really irritating.

Don't add things just because you can.

Put nothing on the screen that gets in the way of your purpose; have things there that reflect your brand values. If in doubt, leave a space.

> **CAUTIONARY TALE**
>
> I asked the same student to tell the group about his website's purpose and how he intended to achieve it. He didn't want his or his colleagues' names or faces on it because he was in IT security. That was fine because he got many of his customers through personal recommendation, through networking and conferences, by meeting them face-to-face. The website was there to give a good impression of his organisation, to build his brand identity. But he did say that he wanted a very fancy Flash introduction, one of those animations which load up and move around impressively but don't actually do anything. Everyone else in the class had said that those things drove them mad because they were a complete waste of time, but he explained that for techies, this is a symbol to show that you're cool, so he wanted one. For his customers, a time-wasting, bandwidth munching intro was what they needed to reassure them that they'd come to the right place. A Flash introduction shows people that your site has been built by professionals. It's a symbol.

Given the chance, all techies will throw in a Flash introduction or a moving object on the page to demonstrate their professionalism, and most customers aren't impressed because these things are a barrier to information they want. So before someone is determined to add this feature to your site, ask yourself what your site's visitors want. Do they need to be impressed by the people who built it, or by you? If it gets in the way of your purpose, don't be talked into having one.

REAL PEOPLE OR STOCK SHOTS?

We've all seen them, they stalk business-to-business websites and brochures: pictures of attractive people smiling into a telephone or staring seriously at a computer screen. They all look as if they bought their clothes and had their haircut in the mid 1990s and are often far too good-looking but not sufficiently intelligent for the job they appear to be doing.

This is one of those things you should question. Why do companies do this? Because that's what other people do. A more creative approach would be to ask, "What can we do differently?"

Do your customers want to know who they are really dealing with, or look at some space-filling photographs that have been bought from a catalogue? What would you rather see when you visit a website yourself?

Have a look at Learn to Dream's website www.

learntodream.co.uk. Click on "Our Company" and then "Meet the Staff". Visit Shelton Fleming at www.sheltonfleming.co.uk and click on "Talent" (if you can get the irritating Flash to stop moving for long enough). Finally, go to What If! www.whatifinnovation.com and click on "Our People". These are professionally built websites, but all three companies have thought about their brand identities and have done something interesting that helps you to understand them better.

CLIP ART

Avoid it. It looks better to have a big blank space than a 1970s-style cartoon that has nothing to do with your brand identity and values. If you are completely stuck, then stick to one illustrator and one style, simple line drawings or colour. Don't mix up a load of different styles unless you're being ironic.

WRITING FOR THE INTERNET

There's much heated debate about whether or not writing for the internet is the same or different from writing for print. What's important is that it has to be good. Your words should work with the design to make people want to read what you've written, then go and do something you want them to.

Before you start to write, ask yourself what it is you want your reader to do. Your aim could be to get them to do one of these:

- email you
- pick up the phone
- order what you're selling
- recommend what you do to someone else
- put you in a link on their Facebook page
- join your mailing list
- be entertained
- something else

But it's good to have a clear idea of what you want.

There's also a myth that no-one reads anything on the internet. Not true. No-one reads badly written copy that's boring, tedious and uninspiring. Make it interesting and don't get bogged down with keywords.

KEYWORDS

We talked about them earlier, but now's the time to explore how to use them. A keyword is a phrase or word you can use to identify what your website or blog is about so that search engines can find them more easily. When you build a web page, there will be a space for you to enter keywords. Getting this right is part of search engine optimisation, which just means making it easy for search engines to find you and put you towards the top of their list of results. We use them to help your website show up on search engines by directing people to the right place. Your keywords should match what you write about yourself in your copy.

If you're building a website for a florist's shop in Leeds, you might list keywords like: flower, bouquet, gift, roses, dozen red roses, flower delivery, bunch of flowers, floral tribute, wedding flowers. But that's going to put you in direct competition with every florist in the world, so you also have to add: Leeds, Yorkshire, Leeds florist, UK. Customers are more likely to write "florist in Leeds" in a search engine than just "florist".

You'll come higher up the search engine list if you put yourself in your customers' shoes and imagine what it is they would search for, then use these words and phrases yourself.

There is an art to writing your web copy so that search engines locate you. When you match the phrases and words you use in your copy with the ones you use as keywords, then intelligent search engines will reward you for not attempting to cheat them by misleading their searches.

Even better is to write so that no-one notices you're including the keywords. If a specialist web writer comes up with copy like this, don't use them:

We're the finest florist in Leeds. If you're looking for a florist in Leeds, then you've found us. Last year we were voted one of the best florists in Leeds by people looking for florists in Leeds.

I only wish I were kidding, but I'm not. There are companies who will take your money for writing copy specifically targeted at search engines, completely forgetting that a human being is going to have to read such tripe.

POTENTIAL PITFALL: SPECIALIST WRITING FOR THE WEB

People who claim to be specialist writers for the internet will occasionally tie themselves in verbal knots trying to cram as many keywords into their copy as they can. Remember your reader. It's all very well to get them on to your website with a lavish scattering of keywords to please the search engines, but if they get there and find that your copy is unreadable, they'll soon move on. Remember that you are writing words to guide machines, but for people to read.

Besides, the way the internet is going at the moment, more people are coming to websites from recommendations in social media like Facebook and Twitter. If the trend continues, keywords become less important.

TOP TIP

Match your words and phrases with the ones your customers would use. If you find yourself using industry terms, edit them out and change them to everyday language. To the outside world, it looks like jargon. Every industry has its own jargon; we are usually familiar with one of them and complete outsiders for all the others.

For example, a financial adviser might use the phrase "financial planning" in his text. His customer would be more likely to search for "savings" or "investments". A company running computing courses might say that they specialise in "learning and development" but their customers think of it as "training".

If your keywords match the ones that customers use in a search engine, you're more likely to get found. You can always use both dialects: professional jargon and everyday language.

YOUR BRAND IN WORDS

There's an area of branding called tone of voice. It's the way that you express your brand's personality in words. There tend to be golden ages in copywriting, then dull plateaux. We're in a golden age at the moment and the web has helped stir it up a bit. You might have come across designers saying, "No-one reads long copy because it's boring." That's rubbish, but it became a self-fulfilling prophecy. Writers didn't bother to put anything interesting in the details, because they thought it was a waste of time if no-one was going to read it anyway. Now, we know that if we make it interesting, people will read it.

Then what happened was that writers started to ignore the "rules" of long copy and write text that was entertaining. Lush and Innocent were at it in the late 1990s, and by the 00s the big brands were at it too: giving their brands a personality, writing like human beings for other human beings to read.

POTENTIAL PITFALL:
COMPLICATED LANGUAGE

What goes wrong is that people think they have to write the way others have always written.

You get things like: "In order to prevent any potential damage in transit, it is essential to maintain the correct orientation."

What that really means is: "Keep this the right way up and it'll get there safely."

There's a huge resistance to stripping out all the complicated words that don't need to be there, because their writers feel that it makes them look intelligent when they write like that. They are comfortable when they pad out their language with long words. They forget that it's not their job to impress the reader; it's their job to help the reader understand what they mean.

No-one ever listed their brand values as pompous, distant and stuffy. Why do they use that tone to communicate? It doesn't impress; it pushes people away.

Which websites did you enjoy reading when you did your research on Day One? What's good about them? What makes you feel as if they are writing for you and have your interests at heart? How do they sound? Can you picture the person who wrote the words you are reading?

Have a go at writing the first thing that your customers will see when they visit your site. Imagine what you would say to the ideal customer you described on Day Two if you met them face-to-face. Then write that down. Here's a space for it.

DIY OR PS?

Most of us can write. In the past, you could get through a whole career in management without having to dictate more than the occasional letter, or write an annual report. Now, we all have computers and do a lot of the writing ourselves.

If you know you're quite good at it, give it a go. If you don't have time, or you know that you never quite manage to write what you really want to say, use a copywriter. A good place to find one is the 26 website at www.26.org. uk, and I'm not just saying that because I'm a director.

At the end of the book, there's a reading list for people who would like to improve their business writing.

The single most important thing to remember is that a person is going to be reading it. Start with a pen and paper, or an open word processing document; when you're new to this, it will take a few tries before you are certain you are ready to publish what you've written. The most experienced copywriters still make mistakes.

PROOFREADING

Reuse paper printed on one side to print out your copy and check it offline. Even the current computer generation learned to read on paper, so most of us find it easier to proofread on paper than on screen. If you have someone who'll proofread it for you, take advantage. It's almost impossible to spot the mistakes in your own work, because you know what you were intending to write, so your brain doesn't always spot your errors. (I had a terrible habit of typing "manger" instead of "manager" and as a spell-checker only picks up words that don't exist, not the ones that are in the wrong place, it got into a couple of important documents.)

"It has to come from your heart — your words and expressions — otherwise it can be off-brand, and the language a writer uses may jar. For people to be excited about your business, you have to be excited too! Blogs, newsletters, bulletins — all the personal stuff that allowed the passion in your business to come through — do that yourself." — Sarah Pierce, Merchants of Vino

POTENTIAL PITFALL: GRAMMAR AND PUNCTUATION

Getting it right is about politeness. If your website is well written and correctly punctuated, that makes it easier for your customers to read. It's that simple. No-one notices if you get your spelling, punctuation and grammar right. If you're not sure, you risk annoying people. A badly written email gives the impression that you don't really care about getting things right. If you can get your passion down on paper, but aren't sure about your spelling and grammar, at the very least get a writer to check it, and if you can afford it, get them to tweak it for you or rewrite the whole thing in your brand's tone of voice. It doesn't have to cost a fortune. Ask a writer if they'll spend an hour on it for you, and if this takes out some daft errors, it might save you some lost customers.

All the above applies to the next day's topics too.

DAY
5

GETTING THE BEST FROM
SOCIAL NETWORKS

Why bother with social networks?

They remind people that you exist, just like advertising and PR, but on a smaller scale and it's free. If you write or post links, pictures or illustrations about something sufficiently attention-grabbing, you'll get people following what you say. At that point, it becomes a powerful communications tool.

But there are other ways to use blogs and social media than just publishing your own views and opinions. You can use them for research, for instant information about what's happening in your market or your world, and for PR. It's true that millions of people use Facebook and Twitter to send seemingly pointless messages to their friends, but no-one's making you read them and you don't have to use it that way yourself,

If you want lots of people to read what you write, it helps if you're famous or if you're a large organisation; if you're not, you have to try harder, but isn't that always the way? Don't let that hold you back.

"I sometimes question Twitter's value (investment of time rather than money), but I'm slowly starting to reap the rewards of persevering."
— Emma Runciman

What you can use social networks for:
- Telling the world what you're up to
- Finding out what's happening right this minute
- Having influential people describe what you do
- It's quite good fun!

One reason that social media and blogs weren't initially embraced or handled well by big organisations was that people used them for entertainment, so companies didn't take them seriously, but now they are getting the hang of it. If you've got a teenager at home who spends all her spare time on Facebook, you might not be so keen when someone suggests that you use it for the serious business stuff. Don't let that put you off. Some organisations do all their online marketing just by using Facebook pages and LinkedIn networks. But if it's not for you, no-one's going to force you into it. It's one more tool in your online marketing kitbox.

How do you make Facebook, Twitter and a regular blog help you? It's that list again. Make them:
- interesting
- useful
- entertaining
- valuable
- amusing
- and preferably a combination of at least two of those things

TOP TIP

There was a great blog post on the Marketing Sentinel site recently, comparing Lush and The Body Shop's use of social media. Why do Lush, a smaller private company, do so much better than The Body Shop, owned by L'Oreal and with much bigger budgets? On their Facebook status that morning, The Body Shop said, "Hello to all our UK fans! Be sure to join the The Body Shop UK fan page for more on our latest campaigns, promotions, competitions and special events near you: http://facebook.com/thebodyshop." Lush's said, "It's a busy morning here in Lush, how's everyone else doing today?"

No prizes for guessing which company has ten times more followers than the other. Lush was really talking to its customers, and they joined in the dialogue. The Body Shop was sending them somewhere else and not expecting anyone to get back to them.

To make it work for you, you've got to be prepared to put the effort in. Try it, and if you love it, keep going. But do give it a try because it's about to topple search engines from their number one slot as a way to bring new people to your website. (By the time you read this, it might already have happened.)

> If you are going to use social media, be sociable.

Before you start writing, remind yourself why you are doing it. You want people to read from the start to the finish, and then do something.

Ask yourself what it is you want them to do, before you write. What is your aim?

It could be to call you, to click a link, to remember

that you exist, or to get to know, understand or trust you better, ready for when you want them to do something serious, like spend their money with you.

Only one thing is certain about social networking, and it's that there'll be a few new ones up and running by the time you read this. But Facebook, LinkedIn, Twitter and YouTube have reached critical mass and will still be important. MySpace evolved to be the natural home of bands and musicians. If that's you, concentrate on that one first.

Here is a guide to getting started on the current biggies.

FACEBOOK

www.facebook.com

You can't get a look at it unless you have a Facebook profile of your own, or unless you sit next to someone who already uses it and lets you watch what they're up to.

Facebook started as an online updatable yearbook for graduates of Harvard and Yale. Look at it now and you'd never believe it. Again, there's no point giving you exact instructions for what to click where, because its owners keep redesigning it.

But this is what you'll need to get going. Have a digital photograph of yourself handy on your computer to use as your profile picture. If you don't have a photograph up, then everyone will know you're not taking it seriously.

Getting started:

- To set up your own profile, go to www.facebook.com
- Pick a user name; your own name is best. Later, you can set up a page for your organisation that everyone on Facebook can look at — whether they are linked to you as your "friend" or not — and you can build it a profile too.
- Choose a password. Make it long with letters in upper and lower case, numbers and some punctuation and write it down somewhere just in case.
- Use the search box to find people you know; make sure they are the right ones. (I'd counted 110 Sarah McCartneys before I got bored with it.) Click the box "Add as friend". You get the option to add a personal message. Fingers crossed, your friends will accept. Once you're there, you'll get requests back again. Accept or ignore. Building up a collection of friends doesn't happen on the first day. Keep going over the next few weeks to get an idea, and months to build up a presence.
- When you visit your home page, your friends' status updates — the short notes that they post about what they are up to — will appear in your news feed, a live update of what's happening.
- To add or take away personal details, click "Profile" at the top right of the screen. Then click on "Info"

and look for the little "Edit" buttons with a pencil graphic next to them. Click those to change things.

• To control who sees what, click on "Account", then scroll down to "Privacy Settings" to edit them.

Right, that's you all set up. Go back to "Home". The Facebook developers keep changing this, but at the moment there is an option to see the "Most Recent" and "Top News" updates. Popular ones are those that other people have commented on or "liked" by clicking the "Like" button.

HANDY HINT: HOW TO GET RID OF ALL THE TRIVIA FROM YOUR NEWS FEED

If your friends use Facebook apps (applications, like games or horoscopes), every last detail gets posted on your news feed. But you can get rid of these without giving up your Facebook friendships. Where you see a friend's name, move your cursor to the right until a blue cross appears. Click on it. You get the option to hide that person or to hide the app they are using. Click on the name of the app. If one of your friends drives you bonkers, but you don't want to offend them by "unfriending" them, you can click "Hide" and their posts won't show up on your page.

Have a look at the kind of things other people write, then join in. If you write on your friends' "walls" or comment on their posts, remember that all their friends can read them too. Some people prefer not to be Facebook friends with their parents or children for just that reason.

> **POTENTIAL PITFALL: SECURITY**
> Anywhere that's popular online attracts internet baddies; they try to hack (hijack) accounts and use them to direct people to their own websites. There's also the danger that, if you give away too much information about yourself, you could be making it easy for people to steal your online identity.
>
> You can hide your date of birth. On Facebook, you can also limit your access to friends or friends of friends rather than allowing every user to have a look at your page. Some people will be Facebook friends with everyone who contacts them; some prefer to stick with people they actually know.

Setting up your organisation's profile

Organisations can set up their own Facebook pages. To get an idea of what they are like, visit the Facebook pages of a couple of organisations that are getting it right.

Here are a few of my favourites, ones I think are using Facebook well:

- Marmite, with over half a million friends
- Lush, for their competitions and friendliness
- Eurostar, for keeping travellers up to date and treating us like people, not stats
- Highland Tiger, for news on Scotland's wild cats
- Floatworks Flotation Centre (just because I like it)

- Breast Cancer Care, raising their profile in a clear, positive way

To make one for your organisation, put "create a facebook page" into the search box and follow the instructions. They make it very easy for us.

Facebook will encourage you to promote your page by advertising to their users. It works by pay-per-click (PPC) so you can set a limit on how much you are prepared to spend every day and how much you are prepared to pay for someone to click on the link to your page. We'll talk more about this tomorrow.

It's impossible to spend more than you've got, as long as you remember to set your own limits. It's also possible to define the people you want to reach very tightly. For example, if I want to advertise workshops for web copywriting in West London, I can specify that I only want to reach people living in West London who are interested in writing, find out how many of them there are, and add or take away constraints on my target group to make it worthwhile.

See how it works and build yourself a decent page before you start spending money. You can also promote yourself and your page by putting a link to it on your status and by posting on people's walls if you think they'll be interested. (Don't bombard them, or they'll hide or unfriend you.)

With a Facebook page, you can have a business presence online without having to build a web page, but you're restricted to publicising yourself to Facebook users. Even the queen is on Facebook now: www.facebook.com/ TheBritishMonarchy

TWITTER

www.twitter.com

The queen is on Twitter too, but not the real queen. Twitter is a more anarchic place; when it was built, no-one really knew how it would work or what it would be used for. It is made up of a constant stream of short messages of up to 140 characters — called tweets — about everything in the world that's going on at any moment, as observed and commented on by its users. With millions of people using it, that's far too much information for anyone to read at any one time. To make Twitter work for you, you've got to be selective.

You've also got to put the effort in. Signing up and then expecting something to happen, without any input of your own, is like joining a gym and expecting to get fit without doing any exercise.

For the media, it's an amazing live information source.

For businesses and other organisations, it's a place where you can give your customers instant updates, find out if they're happy with you (or not), and see what your competitors are up to.

As an individual, you can use it to find out millions of things, like keeping up to date with friends, getting special offers from shops, keeping up with gossip and searching for the latest travel news; whatever you need is there somewhere.

There's been a public row among the intellectual celebrati, some saying it's a waste of time and others collecting hundreds of thousands of followers by tweeting regularly and amusingly.

As with all the other ideas in the book, the only way to find out if it's going to be useful for you is to try it and then decide for yourself.

Why bother?

If your organisation has a lot to say about itself and you want to send out regular updates, then Twitter is a good place to do it. If you need to keep a close eye on what's happening in your market, you can use Twitter to keep tabs on competitors and other influences on your market.

Who does it? Businesses, famous people, millions of individuals, politicians, pressure groups, charities, journalists.

Who doesn't? If you don't enjoy using Twitter or if it takes you an hour to edit your thoughts into 140 characters, then don't do it.

Who doesn't do it, but appears to? With Twitter,

some users tweet under the guise of famous people, but just do it for fun. One of the funniest pretends to be Queen Elizabeth II, under the name Queen_UK. Some celebrities get their assistants to tweet for them. There are some unintentionally funny posts from celebrities and top businessmen who pretend to write their own tweets, when they are privately known to be completely computer illiterate, but they have good lawyers, so see if you can spot them for yourself as I shan't be naming them.

Quite a few writers I know tweet on behalf of organisations who don't have anyone to do it for them, in their brands' tone of voice. If you decide that Twitter is important, but that you don't want to do it yourself, you can pay a copywriter to tweet in your brand's tone of voice.

Getting started

To sum it up, you can use Twitter for two different things:
1. Finding things out
2. Making things happen

To get the most out of it, you can do both. You can also use it for fun. Starting out, the best way to experience Twitter is to give yourself an hour and explore.

1. Finding things out

Go to Twitter's home page: www.twitter.com

Think of something you'd like information on at this moment. Type that into the search box at the top, press the "search" button and a list of tweets will appear. You can read them, and if you find a tweet with a link to a bigger story, you can click on that to take you to more information.

For your organisation: Look for your competitors and see what they are up to. Use the search box for this too. Put your competitors' names in, or what they do, and see what comes out. You can put in your own organisation's name to see if you have any mentions.

For yourself: This is how Twitter came in handy for me last weekend. We had the in-laws round to watch a football match on an expensive online sports service. It crashed. We spent 20 minutes trying to log on again, rebooting the computer, doing everything we could think of, and I spent 10 minutes on the helpline, shouting pointlessly at a recorded message. I searched on Twitter, putting the name of the channel in the search box, and immediately found more than 20 messages expressing the same frustration. Then one person tweeted a link to the TV company's forum, where we all read a message promising that the engineers were working on it. It was back up in time for the second half.

It's great to be able to find out immediately that it's not just you, and that something is happening.

For the media: Journalists use Twitter for instant information. If someone writing a news story on flooding wanted to find out where there are floods around the world right now, he could go to Twitter's home page, write "floods" in the search box at the top of the page and get a list of tweets that mention floods. Doing this right now, I get news on floods in Indonesia, Ethiopia, Hungary and Pakistan, plus a tweet from a woman whose drama lesson ended in floods of tears. Search engines take you literally; they can't read your mind. You do get the trivial thrown in with the serious, but usually there's plenty of useful information out there to give you what you need.

If you tweet on a newsworthy subject, people will probably find it. If it's useful to them, they'll start to follow your tweets.

Using Twitter for research gives you a picture of just how huge it is, and what a useful source of information it can be.

POTENTIAL PITFALL: AVOIDING THE WRONG LINKS

When you are using Twitter for research, be careful where you click. As you've only got 140 characters, people often use software to change a long link to a specific page on a website into a shorter one. This won't have the website name in it, just a series of numbers and letters, so you can't tell what it is before you click it.

To give you an idea whether or not you are clicking on a safe link, click the picture (icon) at the left of the tweet, or the name of the person who wrote it (in bold next to the picture) and that will take you to their Twitter home page. That way you can check to see that they look like trustworthy people. Read some of their tweets to see if this one is written in their usual style.

Spammers and phishers also hijack people's accounts occasionally. If you know someone and they start to write in a completely unrecognisable style, that's probably because their account has been taken over (hacked) by a baddy. Don't click on anything that is phrased oddly, especially when it's from a friend you know would never write like that.

That said, Twitter's engineers work hard to get rid of timewasters, and you can report anything that looks suspicious by clicking "Report for spam" on their home page in the right hand column in red.

2. Making things happen

Twitter comes under the banner of social networking because you can use it to stay in touch with your friends and family. But it's more than that. You can also observe online conversations and trends. Some comedians' Twitter banter is worth signing up for, even if you're not going to use it for anything else.

By putting @ in front of someone's username, you can send that person a message they'll be able to find, even if they don't follow you. By putting # in front of a subject, you can join in with a worldwide online Twitter conversation on that issue.

Using Twitter to post tweets is also called micro-blogging, for fairly obvious reasons. It's different from Facebook, because everyone can read what you write (unless you choose to keep your posts private and only allow people to follow you by asking permission). It's also different in that Twitter doesn't have to be a two-way relationship.

Following

To make Twitter work for you, you can follow interesting people and build up a collection of followers who want to read your tweets. I say "people" rather than organisations, because within an organisation, it's usually one person who does the tweeting. In bigger organisations, they share it but aim to keep the same tone of voice.

Don't let other people's Twitter use put you off. Observe the wrong person and you'll see carelessly written tweets that say things like: "Im at work." "Todays boring." "Got a nu pair of blu shus." Millions of tweets are this uninspired, which is why many people have got the impression that it's dull. But you can avoid all the Twitter twaddle by choosing who you follow carefully, and only tweeting when you've something useful to say. People who've chosen to devote their precious moments to following you can decide just as quickly to "unfollow" you if you bore them or give them a hard sell, or if you never tweet at all.

Often, when you follow people you know in real life,

they'll follow you back, but only if you continue to interest them. If you're following famous people, it's unlikely that they'll rush to follow you back.

Twitter mythology
It's cool to have more followers than people you follow.

No, it's really not important. It depends entirely why you're using Twitter.

If you're out there to be heard and be influential online, then yes, you want lots of people to follow you. There's also a limit to the time you can spend reading what people write. If you're using it for research, you might follow thousands but only have a few followers of your own. If you're famous, you probably have thousands of followers but choose only to follow people you know.

Getting people to follow you for the right reasons
There are plenty of ways to get people to follow you, but there is no point putting the classic hooks (words like "free", "sex" and "chocolate") in your tweets unless that's what your organisation offers all the time.

- Write about what you do. Don't boast, unless it's with some humour.
- If you want to make a point more than once, make it interesting. Never tweet the same thing twice; bored people unfollow you.
- Learn to write in 140 characters.

- Think about what will be interesting to your readers.
- Give away a few secrets to your competitors.
- Be careful with metaphors. I wrote about writers' tattoos once, describing the ink stains I get on my hands from using fountain pens. I instantly got (and quickly lost) more than 50 tattoo artists. Write about knitting two ideas together and the knitting community will follow you.

Again, if you want people to read what you write, use the list:
- interesting
- useful
- entertaining
- valuable
- amusing
- preferably a combination of at least two of those things

If you get into the habit of posting links to things that are any or all of the above and relevant to your followers, then you'll get a reputation for being reliable and people will take an interest in what you post. This doesn't happen in a day, not even in a week.

If you get too pushy and constantly tweet about nothing but yourself, you'll be "unfollowed".

Unfollowing people

You'll find that you follow some people who tweet every five minutes; that can get so tedious that you'll probably unfollow them very quickly.

To unfollow someone, click on their icon or their name in bold to take you to their home page. Currently, there's a green box that says "Following" with a tick on it. Move your mouse over it and it turns red and says "Unfollow". Click it and their tweets will stop turning up in your Twitter feed.

Retweeting

If you like something you read and you want to share it with other people, you can press the RT button, which puts that tweet into your own messages so your followers can read it. If you write something that's retweeted, that will probably pick you up a few extra followers too.

There are entire books on how to get the most from Twitter; this is just for starters. Get this far and you'll begin to get the hang of it.

LINKEDIN
www.linkedin.com

This is the business side of social networking. LinkedIn call their organisation "the world's largest network of active, influential professionals". If that's your market, then go there and spend your time building your profile. Here's where you link with people you've done business with or with ex-colleagues. It has turned into a great place for recruitment, and you can join common interest groups. You can start with a free version, but if you want to contact people who are unconnected with you within LinkedIn (even if you know them in the real world), you have to subscribe to upgrade your account.

Like Facebook, you can update your status; here, people generally write about their work, not what they're doing once they've left for the evening.

If your customers are business organisations, then it's worth setting up a profile in LinkedIn and maintaining it, creating your own online business network by finding people you know. Recommend them, and get recommendations in return.

You can use your LinkedIn profile to describe your organisation and to find people you've worked with and make contact again. Again, it reminds people that you're around and tells them what you're doing.

But as with Facebook, there is the opportunity to advertise what you do to other LinkedIn members. On my page today, I got ads for an executive MBA course, business books on Amazon, a selection of jobs, and some posh hats. They are beginning to promote advertising to their members; what they have is a strong network of business professionals, a valuable resource.

LinkedIn is more about you than your organisation.

Now you've got the hang of setting up a profile, you'll find LinkedIn just as simple as the others.

Visit Facebook, Twitter and LinkedIn. Get recommendations from friends and people in your area of work about which networks they are using. Try them and choose a couple to devote your attention to, because if you try to take on too many, there'll be no time left for working.

With social networking, you've got to keep at it to have an impact. So pick the ones that will work best for you and drop in regularly with your news.

DAY
6

MAKING CONNECTIONS AND BRINGING IN VISITORS

It's true that by having your own website everyone in the world can see you, but not everyone will want to do business with you. We all need to know who our customers are likely to be and where we'll find them.

There are as many ways to market your organisation on the internet as there are websites, and there are plenty of companies keen to sell you the means to do it. It's akin to the 1849 San Francisco gold rush. Who made the money? The people selling shovels and cooking breakfast. Now, there's a boom in SEO because it's tempting to take them up on it when you're doing all the hard work building a business, and someone comes along and promises to make it easier for you by selling you new tools and guaranteeing to make you successful. Think twice before you spend the money, because it depends on your organisation and your aims.

It's great to invest in search engines to promote your online business when you're selling downloadable music files, software or something that's easy to post or email around the globe. If you're promoting your gardening services, café, one-to-one financial advice, yoga centre, farmer's market, business consultancy, art classes or any situation where you and your customers have to be in the same place at the same time, then you have to look for your business in other ways too. SEO is not the only answer, besides you or your web designer can do most of it yourself; you don't necessarily need to pay consultants.

Without planning exactly what you want to achieve and who you want to reach with your online marketing, you might as well take your cash, fold it into paper boats and set them off at the nearest beach. Do the planning first, and you'll spend both your time and money more effectively.

At the moment, there are four main ways to bring people to your website:

- social media (covered on Day Five)
- search engines
- email marketing (more effective with an older market)
- all the other stuff you do in the real world

Sort out your priorities before you pile all your resources into one of them.

The various social media are poised to topple search engines off the top slot for their ability to bring new visitors to websites. People will follow a link to a website from someone they know on Facebook or Twitter as it is closer to a personal recommendation than a search engine technological algorithm. Search engines lack human warmth and emotion, and we'd still rather get advice from a person than a machine. I will follow links from people whose opinions I value, so I'm likely to click on a link from their tweets or status updates just to see what's there.

CONNECTING WITH YOUR CUSTOMERS

One of my favourite websites is The Writing Desk www. thewritingdesk.co.uk, because when I'm not using a computer, I write in notebooks with refillable fountain pens, modern and vintage. At The Writing Desk, you can buy ink in hundreds of colours, pens, pencils, paper, notebooks and other beautiful things. This week, I went there to buy a bottle of highlighter ink and a modestly priced broad nibbed pen to use it in. I'm tired of throwing away plastic highlighter pens; this should last me forever. However, what I didn't like was that you had to tick everything twice to make sure you'd bought it. It drove me bonkers. I could get to the check-out and find that I'd left a bottle of lavender ink behind somewhere and have to go back and find it, tick it, then tick that I'd picked the right thing before it was added to my basket.

Why do I keep going there? Because I like the products. I get a monthly newsletter, and I usually visit the site when it arrives. I know they have things I want. It's a small, specialist company run by two dedicated people, and although I only know them through the website, I feel as if I'm connected to them. Websites are not as anonymous as marketing people imagine; they are a close connection between customers and businesses. If you feel that connection, then you'll continue to do business. It's not all about technology; it's also about creating a bond. And now they've fixed the thing with the ticks, so I like it even better.

How do you connect with the websites you like? How often do you use search engines? When do you follow links that people have recommended? How often do you open email newsletters and click on their links? Do you visit websites after you've met some of their people face-to-face? Here's a space for notes.

SEARCH ENGINE OPTIMISATION: KEYWORDS

Online marketing often focuses on how to bring people to your website using search engines. There are huge sums spent — and earned — in search engine optimisation (SEO), but that's not the only way to do it, and it might not be relevant for your business. Don't let someone talk you into pouring hundreds or thousands into an SEO strategy before you've decided what it is you need.

Besides, if you have a designer to help you build your site, they will take care of your SEO for you as part of the price.

SEO is all about how to get to the relevant front page on search engines like Google and its pals when someone is looking for an organisation that does what you do. Of course, SEO is crucial when the main way that new people find you is through search engines, but if you get your business though personal recommendations, you should be spending your time and money on meeting more people, not handing it over to an SEO consultancy.

Here's a typical — and real — email from a consultancy you probably wouldn't want to use:

"Hello and Good Day!
"I am Stela, Business Development Manager, with a reputed online marketing company.

I was surfing through your website and realized that despite having a good design; it was not ranking on any of the search engines for most of the keywords pertaining to your domain.

I was wondering if you would be interested in getting the SEO done for your website.

There is a simple equation that is applicable to the online world.

Ethical SEO -> Better Traffic -> Higher Sales

SEMPO is a registered Online marketing firm and have over 5 years of working experience. All the techniques used are ethical and proprietary.

In case you require any additional information, it shall be our pleasure to furnish the same.

So let me know if you would like me to mail you more details or schedule a call. We'll be pleased to serve you.

I look forward to your response."

I get a couple of these every day. After a while, you start to wonder if they are right and you're doing something wrong, but then you realise that it's spam, and most of them haven't looked at your site at all.

Thousands of consultancies will promise to get you on to the front page of Google for your category. There are 10 slots. Be reasonable. These people earn their fees from organisations who have been persuaded that it will make or break their business to be at the top of the rankings. There are books on online marketing and SEO that promise you thousands of new customers and a fortune of "literally" countless millions if you get to the top of the Google rankings. Piffle. One book I read threatens that if you fail with your Google advertising, "you will be killed". Really, it says that. You won't be killed. It won't even kill off your business. The important part is to make sure that for each euro, pound, yen or dollar you spend on your online marketing, you get a good deal more back. Do not give in to the bullies, and question anyone who promises you unreasonable results.

Besides, of all the people I know who run their own organisations, only one wants to build his business, sell out and make millions; the others would like to continue doing what they do, with a bit more income and a bit less stress. If they suddenly increased their business by a factor of ten, they'd have to turn 80% of it down.

In the web world, if someone starts selling hard and wants to sign you up for a six-month contract or longer, offering you a deal that's only available "today", view it with the scepticism that you would if they were trying to sell you any other product. This happens with unscrupulous paid-for online directories, SEO companies and pay-per-click advertising consultants.

That said, making sure that your website and blog have the right keywords in place is a sensible thing to do. If someone is looking for you on a search engine, this will help them to find you. And there are many ethical, reputable SEO consultants who will help search engines and customers to find you. But it's not that hard; refine your keywords to match the things your customers are likely to search for, match your online copy to your keywords and off you go.

Go back to Day One, to the place where you wrote down your search words and phrases. Use these.

We're going to get slightly techie for a moment: meta tags. People who design websites will talk about these. In the old days of the internet, search engines seemed to send you on meaningless diversions to websites that had nothing to do with what you'd put in the search box. You could put "BBC" or "New York Times" in the box and get directed to a site selling counterfeit handbags or worse. That's because some website owners would cheat and build popular search terms into their web pages' invisible structure (meta tags) to mislead early search engines into thinking that this was what the site was all about.

Google quickly became successful because it ignored these meta tags and only read websites' keywords, which it then matched with the copy to check that they said similar things. Then they would dump all the cheats right to the bottom of the rankings and bury them so deep that they were never found again. They still do this; if your keywords don't match your copy, you can be slammed into the deep, dark Google dungeon and it can take you years to get out again. You won't even appear if you are a sweet shop on Acton High Street and someone puts "Acton High Street Sweet Shop" into the search box, not until you've proved that you've mended your ways. It is in the search engines' interests to deliver the results that their users are looking for. Help them to do that, and you'll be rewarded with a higher rank on the search engine ladder.

Most people only look at the first page, and almost all never make it past three pages, so if it is important to you to be found easily by complete strangers, follow the rules.

CAUTIONARY TALE

A web designer friend of mine has a client who was already spending a fair monthly sum on Google Adwords — paid-for keywords that boost you to the paid-for section on the front page of a relevant search — because it's important for him to bring in a constant flow of new customers to his site. My friend got a call from this client, who said that he'd just paid a fee to a business that promised to get his company to the top of Google's rankings. My chum explained that this was all covered and that was the reason that he already appeared high up the lists and was getting lots of new customers. Then the client's site went to the top of the Google list in his category for two days and disappeared without a trace. The smart Google system had caught them and punished them. Google is programmed by people who want to beat cheats; when their system finds one, a real person then banishes it to search engine obscurity.

So when you come to the place to put your keywords on your site or your blog, filter them so that you put in exactly what your customers will be looking for. Don't use broad terms that will pick up everyone in your entire market. That way, you'll be competing with a far smaller group of competitors, the list will be shorter, and you'll be higher up the rankings.

For example, if you are a financial copywriter in Leeds looking for clients in Leeds, don't just write "copywriter"; put "financial copywriter in Leeds". Clients will find you more easily if you can try to read their minds; think about narrowing your keywords' scope to match the precision of your potential customers' searches.

EMAIL MARKETING

With email marketing, the first step is getting your messages into people's inboxes, the second is getting them to open them, and the third is getting them to pay attention for long enough to do something positive.

Send people a regular email just to remind them that you're there. For not much bother, and very little money, you can reach everyone on your database. It's less intrusive than calling and less expensive than posting a letter. Email marketing is one of the simplest and cheapest ways to stay in touch with your customers and to let them know what's new.

You can send different emails and test them to see

which ones work best. You can divide your customers into different groups and send them different messages. On quiet days, you can bring in extra business.

Each week, I send a small group of people a reminder about yoga classes; if for some reason I don't send it, only half of them turn up. The first time I sent an email to everyone on my website mailing list, Rachel, who built the site, called me and asked what on earth had happened because the hits (visitor numbers) were going through the roof.

I know an organisation that once sent out an email newsletter that had nothing in it at all; they'd pressed "send" accidentally. All it had were the details at the bottom. Customers clicked on it anyway because it reminded them that they rather liked visiting the website when the newsletter arrived; it always had a link to new stuff, so they knew what to expect.

I'm not suggesting that you send empty newsletters; I'm saying that people get into habits, and if you send them something interesting that appeals to them, and if you do it regularly so they come to expect it, they'll probably get into the habit of clicking through to your site.

If you send them something dull, it won't take them long to get into the habit of deleting it.

Sending email from your own computer

First, give yourself an email identity that your customers will recognise.

For example, if you're sending an email from Jane Bell at the Shoe Shop, set up your email account so when it arrives in a customer's inbox, it doesn't just say it's from "Jane"; it says "Jane at the Shoe Shop".

To do this, go to Tools, then Account, then User Information, then Name, and change yours to something that identifies you easily, like "Jane at the Shoe Shop", as we were saying.

In the Subject line, instead of just writing "News", write "News about Shoes".

That way, each week or month, when Jane's email turns up amongst all the other thousands, her customers will think, "Great! Shoe news! I'll open it!" instead of "Who's Jane?" and deleting it.

Next, make it interesting.

It can be short. It can be long. Just make it good. Like we said earlier, there's a myth that no one reads long copy any more, especially not on the internet. That really depends on how interesting it is. Tell stories, make it fascinating, make it funny. Don't waste people's valuable time waffling on about things you think are important; ask yourself what they want to know, and tell them. Cut out all the extra bits. People will scroll down to see what's at the end, but only if the beginning is interesting.

Again, if you want someone to read what you've written, make it:

- interesting
- useful
- entertaining
- valuable
- amusing
- preferably a combination of at least two of those things

Spam filters are set up to intercept and stop emails to groups of people, to avoid the tidal wave of unwanted rubbish from flooding our inboxes. When you get to the point that you are emailing 100s of people rather than 10s, it's time to upgrade to an email marketing package.

The legal side of customer data (see Day One)

As email marketing involves keeping customers' details on your own computer and sending them information, there are quite a few important rules to follow to stay on the right side of the law.

You can find everything you need about the legal regulations for sending business emails at your government's business website. There are some essential points that will keep you out of trouble, and also keep you in your customers' good books, and their address books too.

- All EU countries must follow the 1995 Directive "Directive 95/46/EC on the protection of individuals with regard to the processing of personal data and on the free movement of such data" which stated that each member state must have a law in place by the end of 1998, but each country's rules are different. The laws in Germany and France are particularly firm.

- In the UK, you must follow the 1998 Data Protection Act. If you store any personal details about your customers, above their basic name and address data, then you must register. It is your customers' right to be able to inspect the data that you hold on them to check that it is correct.

- The US is less restrictive than the EU, with no single law covering the range that the EU 1995 Directive encompasses. Laws vary state to state, so it's important to brush up on your local restrictions in the US as well as the EU.

- You must allow everyone you email to opt out of receiving your email and to be taken off your list if they ask you. Give an email address that they can write to, or use an automated system. Even if it isn't law in your country, it is internet common practice and people are less likely to trust emails from an organisation that doesn't follow the usual guidelines.

- Your company name and trading address must be on every email.

- You must keep your customers' email addresses private. In the early days of the internet, companies would put a list of email addresses in the "To:" section, giving everyone on the list access to private email addresses. It still happens occasionally. Always use the "BCC" box if you are going to send out a group email, no matter how small it is.

- You must not send emails to people who haven't asked for them.
- When you send out an email on behalf of your organisation, you've got to make it clear that it's a commercial message, not a personal one.

The perils of spam

You might be saying to yourself, "Hang on a moment; I get masses of emails that don't follow those rules." You're right, of course. There are billions of emails sent every day that break the law. As fast as the internet security programmes are updated to keep out illegal emails, the spammers invent different ways to get around them.

There are some dangerous ones that invite you to click on a link or open an attachment that will take you straight to a site or open a programme that will read information from your computer, steal your saved passwords and could even get into your financial details if you leave too much data hanging around.

The simple rule: if you're not absolutely sure about it, don't open it.

Your potential customers are constantly receiving

illegal emails and deleting them. As usual, the baddies spoil it for the rest of us. Don't give up; don't let them bully you out of sending your own emails, because they can work wonders. To make yours work, they have to be consistent, clear and obviously from your organisation.

POTENTIAL PITFALL: PHISHING

Phishing is pretending to be a reputable company in order to collect sensitive information.

Spamming is sending out thousands of emails to people who haven't asked for them.

You can't stop phishing emails. Not even the banks, eBay, the BBC or Amazon can stop them, but you can learn how to spot them.

For a start, they are usually addressed to "Dear customer" instead of you personally. Sometimes, there are mistakes with the grammar, spelling and use of language. One of my favourites claimed to come from BBC News and invited me to click on a site where I could see the news story "President of Russia has dead."

As soon as you have an email address, it will be copied and used to send out emails for fake prescription drugs, handbags, pornography sites and anything else that the easily led want to buy cheaply. That's unfortunate, but it's going to happen, so don't be surprised when it does.

But there are ways to help your emails reach your customers and encourage them to click and open them.

Get your language right. As well as giving your customers something interesting to read, get your spelling and grammar spot on; that way you can distinguish yourself from the spammers and phishers out there.

Go to websites that you like and subscribe to their emails. Get inspiration from what you enjoy receiving. My own favourite is a long, very witty weekly email from silicon.com. It's called the Weekly Roundup and it's full of stories from the world of IT. It's great, even if you don't think you're interested in the subject; that's the kind of interesting email we all should aspire to send.

Using Email Marketing Tools

Two good ones are Mail Chimp and Constant Contact. With Mail Chimp, you can start small and free. You can design your own email newsletter templates, and if you already tried a blog and a website on Day Three, you'll know how easy that is. You can also add your contacts to a database, put them in a list and divide them into separate groups, if you want to.

One great thing about email marketing tools is that they have bright people working on ways to help your emails go into your customers' inboxes and not get shooed away by spam filters or shoved into the junk file.

Again, search online and look for others that suit your needs if these two don't do the trick.

For a mass of valuable help on email marketing, follow Anna Penrose's blog www.mail-away.co.uk/blog.

If you plan to pay someone to take it all out of your hands, companies like MailAway will do it all for you.

"Emotionally unsubscribed" is a term that Anna Penrose uses to describe getting emails from something you subscribed to years ago, but you never open or read. You can't quite get around to going in there and pressing the "unsubscribe" button, but you don't read them.

Consider the ones you get that make you feel that way. Why do you never open them? What makes you want to open the ones you do? Have a look at your email inbox and do this exercise to give you some insight into what it is that makes an email worth opening. Then use it in your own emails.

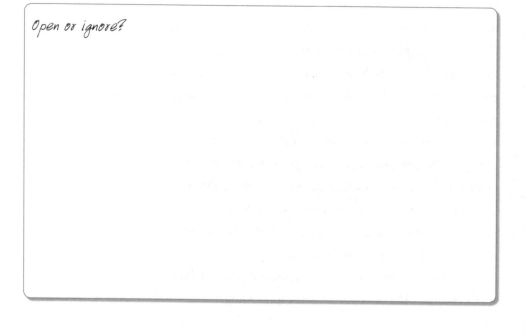

Open or ignore?

DIRECTORIES

Good directories to use are free ones that your trade organisation has set up, if you belong to one. Register your details there, whether you have a website or not, and you've got an online presence included in the price of your membership, and the professional recommendation that goes with belonging to your trade body, if you have one. I'm with www.26.org.uk; it costs me £26 a year and I have already had more business from being found in the members' pages than it will cost me to be there for the rest of my life.

There are thousands of online directories on which you can buy a listing, and teams of salespeople who'll call you to get you to subscribe. Coincidentally, they often happen to have one last space and a special discount that they can give you if you sign up by the end of the day. I've yet to meet anyone who has got good value from using one of these. And the small print can be vicious: if you don't give them three months' notice, you can be subscribed for the following year too.

Another good way to attract the right kind of customer is to search online for relevant free directories you can sign up to. Often, these sites make their money from pay-per-click advertising (see Day Seven) rather than charging for a listing, so they want to encourage as many visitors as they can. You'll benefit from being there.

Check that it reflects your brand values; there are some

sites where you wouldn't want to be seen, no matter how many visitors they get.

COMMUNICATIONS IN THE REAL WORLD

Your online marketing works best if it adds to all your other communications. Before you spend money online, ask yourself what your website is for. Go back to Day Two and remember your purpose. Why do you want to be online? Who are your potential customers and what are the best ways to reach them?

All the research and planning you did at the beginning of the week will be useful if you're intending to work in traditional media too. Your brand values should be exactly the same in the virtual and real worlds, so all your marketing thinking and your communications help to bring your organisation new customers and keep current ones.

If it's PR in the national press or local radio, networking events, leaflets, radio ads or speaking at conferences, then continue to do that. Do as Chas Walton says below and put your web address on everything.

One client recently told me that he was about to spend hundreds on SEO. Then he told me that he gets all his clients by personal recommendation. I stopped him.

As we said earlier, SEO can be great to bring in thousands of new customers to an online shop or a charity or a campaigning group that wants its message broadcast, but if you deal face-to-face with your customers, you'll want to use another route to reach them. That can include online work, like remembering to put your location in your keywords. But it still means that you should take advantage of local media and networking events. Word-of-mouth is still the best source of new customers; it can be online, but unless your organisation operates entirely online, meeting people face-to-face is still the best way to decide if you want to do business with them.

QUICK TIPS

Here are some views — some of them completely contradictory — from people who've tried different ways to bring people to their websites. The point is that everyone needs a different strategy because their aims vary. See what works for you; be open to advice, but don't let anyone push you into spending money before you're certain it's going to help you to achieve your purpose.

"Print your web address on everything. Go networking." — Chas Walton, www.textwizard.com

"Contact everyone you have ever met." — Claire Carroll, www.clairelouisecarroll.com

"Use forums relevant to your business. You get to develop a relationship with potential customers and get feedback on various aspects of the product/ service easily. It also allows for direct contact with the customer on an informal level. Keep the meta tags updated on your website and your website content fresh as much as possible on a daily basis to help with search engine rankings. Make sure you're active on social networks such as Facebook and Twitter and the new ones which are no doubt on their way. It helps to spread the brand and company message directly to customers and followers." — Hossay Momand, www.yllume.com

"Articles strategically placed on high-volume sites" — Anonymous contributor to the research

"Do your own "SEO" by speaking at conferences and use LinkedIn to raise your profile." — Anon.

"Twitter's been building over time — starting to see a bit of momentum now." — Pete Cornes, www. pilcrow.co.uk

"Update content regularly to give people a reason to re-visit your site." — Anna Penrose, www.mail-away. co.uk

"Don't waste time wondering if it might work for you — give it a go." — Emma Runciman, http://thinksaydo.co.uk

"Register with your professional association's directory." — Sarah McCartney, www.symmetry counselling.co.uk

"Promote yourself on industry-specific websites." — Tony Rowlands, www.ajrowlands.com

"Facebook and LinkedIn for freelance connections, reminding clients I exist!" — Lucie Gray, www.facebook.com/lucie.gray

DON'T WASTE YOUR TIME AND MONEY ON...

"Paid-for directories" — Chas Walton

"Expensive brochure websites. The jury is still out on blogs." — Sarah Pierce, www.merchantsofvino.com

"Pay-per-click. You can sign up to all sorts of free advertising groups which boost your web profile." — Ally Hill, www.sarva.co.uk

"Not sure about the value of LinkedIn. Can't tell if it works." — Claire Carroll

"Investing in having a website built too early, before you've decided on the direction the business will take. Don't waste money on SEO, particularly if budget is low; don't go down that road." — Hossay Momand

"Facebook and most social networking" — Anon.

"Things you don't have any appetite for. If you don't enjoy blogging, don't run a blog. If you can't be bothered with Twitter, don't tweet." — Pete Cornes

"Avoid anything until you know it is right for you. Shop around and ask questions to everyone. There are a lot of cowboys online." — Anna Penrose

"Just because everyone says 'you must be on Facebook' doesn't mean you have to — it might just not be right for your business. It's not for mine (at the moment!)" — Emma Runciman

"Pay-per-click. You need to spend serious money for them to be effective." — Tony Rowlands

DAY
7

**EVEN MORE WAYS TO GET
PEOPLE INTERESTED**

SEO TECHNIQUES — INBOUND LINKS & ACTIVE SITES

An inbound link is a link from someone else's web page to yours. The more you have, the higher the search engines' magic wands will put you up the rankings in your categories. Search engines let loose their techie detectives and send them off to explore absolutely every site on the web. They're fast, but it can still take days to report home, so sometimes it can take a couple of days for search engines to find brand new sites after you've published them.

They also search for copy that matches keywords and most important of all, they look for inbound links. In effect, that's one site being recommended by another site. If the search engines find that you are being recommended, then they take it that yours is interesting, reliable and has something that their users will want to know about.

That's one good reason why you should use Facebook, Twitter, LinkedIn and the like and put your own URL in your profile. You can also write about yourself on the social networks and add a link to new things on your site or your blog. Don't do it on every single tweet or update, because then people will hide or block you. If you do anti-social things on social networks, no-one will like you. Like in real life, if you go in there with a hard sell, you'll lose your friends.

Inbound links from sites that have been online for a long time are the most effective. So as my site, www.little-max.co.uk, has been there since 1997 courtesy of Offworld Industries, a link from me and the other old-timers will rate higher than one someone set up last week. It's the search engines' algorithms' method of determining authenticity, of tracking down where real people are running a genuinely useful site.

POTENTIAL PITFALL: BLOG SPAM

One of the reasons you'll get a lot of rubbish posted on a new blog is that borderline-legal professional spamming companies will pay people to sit at computers 24 hours a day, find places they can post without registering and stick idiotic messages on there, including their URLs, in the hope that no-one will notice and delete them.

Here are a couple of examples posted on a blog that I maintain:

"Substantially, the post is actually the sweetest topic on curing acne naturally. I concur with your conclusions and will thirstily look forward to your future updates."

"Thank you a lot for this! I havent been this thrilled by a website for a Extended time! Youve got it, what ever that signifies in blogging. HaHa. Youre undoubtedly somebody that has one thing to say that folks need to hear. Preserve up the excellent work. Preserve on inspiring the men and women!"

As you can tell, they've been turned into bad English by translation software. It's another of the nuisances that come with online activity. If you start a blog, you will have to delete them; it's time-consuming and bothersome, but don't let them stop you. The good guys are working on new ways to block them all the time.

How do you get yourself some inbound links?

- Wherever it's relevant, ask your friends and colleagues to add your site to their useful links section and do the same for them.
- Use social media, and every time you add something new, post a link to it. (But don't go overboard and annoy people with it.)
- Add your site to relevant directories. (I just added my yoga classes to www.yoganearby.com and Google Maps. It's worth a regular search to see what's new.)
- Get yourself written about. Use online PR to get coverage in trade press, newspapers, magazines and blogs. Use press releases about your organisation online the same way you would in the real world, just faster.
- If you post a comment on a blog, make it relevant

and interesting and add your URL. If you don't annoy the owner, then you'll be allowed to stay.

- Join relevant online forums — collections of like-minded people who discuss issues — and after you have been there for a while and contributed in a useful way, let people know where to find you. (Don't barge in there and talk about yourself straight away; that's considered rude and you will suffer the consequences.)
- Be interesting enough for people to post your link on their own pages.

KEEPING BUSY

Update your site regularly and the search engines will notice, report back to base and move you up the rankings. Build a site and forget about it, and you will gradually be overtaken by more active websites.

You don't have to go into the structure and change it every day. You can update your blog or have a Twitter feed that shows up your new posts on your website. Again, if you're not going to update your blog or Twitter regularly, don't have them on your site. It looks a little slovenly when the last update was six months ago, as if someone can't be bothered with the basic housekeeping.

VIRAL MARKETING

There's a difference between hype and buzz, and you've

got to get it right. Buzz is when people start to "talk" about you, to send links to their friends, post links on their blogs or social media profiles, and perhaps the press pick it up. This happened with some of the best Twitter users, who've now got their own book deals. They started for their own amusement and it caught on.

That's why it's been nicknamed viral; it catches on and spreads like a cold, but in a good way.

Hype is when an organisation attempts to force its little film or photograph or ad or blog to go viral and puts a lot of effort into getting people to look at it. If it's none of those things on our list, people will only look at it once and won't recommend it, as that would reflect badly on their good taste.

Every week, Media Guardian publishes a list of the top 10 viral videos at www.guardian.co.uk/technology/series/viralvideochart. Go there and have a look at the latest hits, or go straight to YouTube, www.youtube.com, and watch their recommendations. Also search for "Simon's Cat", just because it's brilliant and did the rounds for that reason.

The best way to illustrate how viral online marketing can work is to let Lorelei Mathias tell her story in her own words:

"The trouble is, 'viral' is a misnomer. You can't insist something you create is 'viral', just by calling it that.

All you can hope is that the idea — whether it's a website, email or book trailer — is interesting enough that people will pass it on.

"Before I was lucky enough to be published, I spent over four years working at Random House as an in-house creative. Everything from big-budget 'Nothing Grips like Grisham' campaigns with giant books stuck to billboards to small-budget 'Super Good Day' stunts with red Beetles for Mark Haddon's *Curious Incident.* One thing which was very clear from doing that job was just how very crowded the market is. It didn't take me long to realise that to make a book stand out these days, you really do have to think of something special.

"When my first book was published in 2006, I knew my publisher (LBD)'s marketing would be brand-led, not author-led. But being an ad creative, I couldn't help thinking of ideas to support it (an occupational hazard). So when my book was picked out for a Waterstones January sale, I couldn't help wanting to do something to help it along — without treading on toes, of course. So I ended up writing a TV script to use online. We couldn't afford to run a TV ad, but I could afford to write one and then use the internet to send it on its journey via YouTube. At the time, YouTube was a pretty much untapped area for book marketing. Back then, the idea of a book trailer didn't really exist, but it's now almost common vernacular.

"Anyway, once I'd written the script, I sent it to the actress, Sarah Smart (from *Wallander*), who I'm a big fan of. She loved the script and very kindly gave her time for the project. (In my dreams, we would both love for her to play the part of Amelie, the novel's heroine, if there was ever a feature film made of it.)

"Many favours later, I managed to get the film produced on a shoestring and put it on YouTube. Once the YouTube trailer and the blog had been organically seeded across chatrooms and friends' inboxes, things took off. The viral had thousands of hits and spread to hundreds of sites and blogs around the globe, everywhere from Croatia to China. It's also led to encouraging PR. One review began, 'After seeing the trailer for *Step on it, Cupid*, I just had to give it a read.'

"I also created a fictitious profile on MySpace for Amelie and a blog for 'the world's most reluctant speed-dater'. This was the perfect way for Amelie to spew out all her different neuroses and generally have a rant, and it was a great way to publicise samples of the book. By creating the online identity of Amelie, the world's most reluctant speed-dater, I was then able to dot her around all the networks and dating chatrooms, so that people clicked on her out of curiosity and were led to the book by her ad-that-didn't-look-like-an-ad. The response was brilliant, with hundreds of new invitations from 'friends' for Amelie, and comments being added to the blog from other speed-daters.

"I was fortunate to win Campaign of the Quarter at the Book Marketing Society, which led to a lot more spin-off PR in *Publishing News* and *The Bookseller*, and a talk at the London book fair. And bizarrely, there are kind comments on blogs calling it 'the best trailer for a book ever!', which is kind!

"Oh and there was also a spike in my Amazon sales ranking. But that said, I don't believe the value in a 'viral' lies directly in sales — it's more about generating awareness, talkability and that old elixir of publishing: word-of-mouth.

"These days, simply shoving a quote on the book jacket and reproducing it to 4xsheet dimensions isn't going to make enough impact. And while it's common practice for a tube campaign to be binned after two weeks, a YouTube or MySpace page costs nothing in media space and has no time limit. I started this campaign back in 2006 and, while it isn't fresh anymore, it's still live, four years on. It's still being viewed by someone in the world every day. This sort of campaign really is the most direct, cost-effective way for your fictional characters to mingle with your target audience — wherever they are in the world. A poster on the tube can't bring your character to life as vividly as a fluffy pink profile on a real social network, or a short film that dramatises their predicament in a compelling way.

"The really wonderful thing about these brave new marketing methods is that they're all accessible to the author. In some ways, MySpace, YouTube, et al., have really made things more democratic, have levelled the playing field for those with small budgets and big ideas. In an article I wrote for *The Bookseller* back in 2007, I wondered aloud whether, to some extent, power was shifting away from the marketing meeting (like the typical one above in Lost for words) and into the hands of the author, the bloggers and the networkers.

"Four years on, I'd say this is truer than ever. The only difference is that there are now infinitely more online tools to add to the mix. Facebook was in its infancy when I did my viral campaign, but today, there is also Twitter, iPhone apps and all kinds of new-fangled technology that offers yet more power to the author. I can barely keep up with them all! At the moment, I have all my films hosted on my author site, Loreleimathias.com, and I have lots of ideas on how to expand it out. I write a blog for the advertising industry on Campaignlive.co.uk, but any more distractions than that and it's impossible to find time to actually do the writing itself! I'm writing my third book at the moment and I have to exercise some restraint sometimes. I can't help coming up with viral ideas while I'm writing it!

"So, any author thinking of dabbling in self-marketing should be careful of that — it can become addictive."

— Lorelei Mathias

You might not have the resources to put together the campaign that Lorelei did, but you can take advantage of opportunities available to you and make something happen in future.

YOUTUBE

Short films have become the staple of the viral marketing world and YouTube is the main place you'll find them. If videos are good, they can be spread around by sending links in emails, but more usually on blogs, forums, chatrooms and social networking sites. In the previous century, online marketing started with people sending messages as email attachments, but that's old-school now; it clutters up the internet and clogs inboxes with huge files. Videos don't even have to be of great quality; if they tick some of the boxes on our earlier list, they'll get watched and recommended.

If you make a professional film for your own website, it's also a good idea to register on YouTube so you can upload your films there and make them available for the world to see. YouTube make their money from sponsored films and advertising, so we can take advantage of free access. It's something that companies use despite it not fitting exactly with their brand values. Even the BBC put their trailers on YouTube for the UK, because that's where people expect to find interesting short films these days. It's a medium in its own right, and too significant to ignore; millions of people go there daily to watch films on things that interest them.

YouTube isn't the only site that hosts user-generated videos. Photobucket and Flickr, two of the early photo album hosting sites, do too. If you visit Wikipedia www.wikipedia.com and search for "video hosting websites", it will show you an up-to-date international list.

PAID-FOR ADVERTISING

Most web advertising (formerly known as webvertising, but that didn't really catch on) comes in the form of pay-per-click (PPC). You place an advertisement on another website with a link to your own. When someone clicks the ad and arrives at your site, you pay for the privilege. There's also pay-per-view (PPV). That's where you pay for an ad to appear on a web page and you pay for the number of times it appears on screen, regardless of whether or not people click on it. Mostly, you bid to get your ad to appear on screen. You decide how much you are prepared to pay per click, based on what it's worth to your organisation, set a maximum limit and a total budget. If someone else bids more, you don't appear until there's no-one else higher up the waiting list than you.

There are variations on this, but that's the long and the short of it.

Before you pay anything, you have to decide how much it's worth to be seen, or to have people brought to your site.

You can also earn revenue for your own website by "monetising" it, allowing ads to appear on it, and getting paid each time a visitor sees or clicks on them. I've got Amazon ads appearing on one of my blogs, just to see what would happen, but I prefer to keep the others clear because having ads doesn't fit with my brand values.

Many blogs and websites do take ads, because they have so many visitors that it's a good source of income for them. Several companies started out as personal-interest blogs, accepted ads and turned into profitable businesses. It's something to consider, but don't rush into it unless it's important to fund your website with advertising revenue.

Google run two of the largest advertising schemes. Buying Adwords gets your listing into the sponsored sections of Google search pages. They are paid-for keywords, so to use Adwords and other search engines' advertising, you have to use the same guidelines with precise use of words to get the best value from the system. These are the listings at the top, sides and bottom of a page on Google; the ones in the middle are the search results that appear because of well-organised SEO. AdSense is the scheme that places appropriate ads on your website or your blog, according to the tags or copy that you write on your pages, what they call "contextually targeted ads". Google looks for relevant words and sticks an ad on the page for you. If this interests you, click on the Google home page where it says "advertising programmes".

Yahoo and Microsoft run big schemes too. Facebook's is becoming more popular and successful as its user base grows and users register their personal interests so advertisers can target precisely. LinkedIn's scheme is targeted at its own professional members.

If you don't need the money, it's probably better not to clutter up your own site with other people's messages when it's hard enough to get your customers to read your own.

As for advertising on other sites, it's worth setting a budget and dipping a toe in the water, just to see what happens. If your money is better spent on going to networking meetings or printing your own postcards, do that instead.

BLOG PR

If blogs are good, people follow them. If they are really good, they get thousands of followers (readers and watchers who get an update each time the bloggers post something new) and they become influential media. A blogger writing about your organisation can have as great an effect as being written about by the press or talked about on the radio and, even better, there's a link to your site. As more people look for instant information online rather than, say, waiting for a monthly magazine, the power is heading in the bloggers' direction.

If a popular blogger writes good things about your organisation, you benefit in two ways. People will read about you and maybe click on a link to your website, and the search engines will find your inbound link.

As with all media coverage, it could be good or bad and you can't make an independent writer publish positive coverage; all you can do is provide the information they need to write about you, hope they like it and give you a good review.

FROM NOW ON

By now, if you've spent all week putting this book into practice, you'll know enough to make the decisions about what to do yourself, what to leave alone and where you need the experts. This was just the start; there are whole books on things we've covered in half a chapter to get you up and running. There are also amazing resources on the internet that can help you if you know where to look. You can start with Wikipedia, the free online encyclopaedia to help you define what you're looking for, then use the commercial search engines for more details.

If you've read this far but not tried it yet, I hope you'll be feeling a lot more confident about getting out there and trying it. Do go ahead. Do it right and it will be inexpensive, effective and will introduce your organisation to new customers in new markets with less risk than any other approach.

And if you've set up your own website with blog attached and are regularly contributing to Facebook, Twitter and LinkedIn and already have a video going viral on YouTube, keep going.

I wish you the very best of luck.

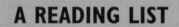

A READING LIST

BOOKS TO HELP YOU WRITE YOUR OWN MARKETING WORDS

We Me Them and It and *The Invisible Grail* by
    John Simmons
Brilliant Copywriting by Roger Horberry

SOME SEARCH ENGINES

www.google.com
www.askjeeves.com
www.bing.com
www.altavista.com

WEBSITES NOT TO BE MISSED

Wikipedia, the fifth largest website in the world, and
the biggest that has been created voluntarily with no
advertising support. It's not always 100% correct, but
it's a great source of information and its editors work
ceaselessly to take out mistakes. It deserves your support

(IMHO) and if you want to read about anything at all, go there. www.wikipedia.com

YouTube: online films. www.youtube.com

The Inspiration Hut. Ideas and inspiration on design, website and blogs. www.inspirationhut.net

26. Not-for-profit association for writers and everyone interested in working with words. An excellent place to find yourself a copywriter. www.26.org.uk

ONLINE MARKETING ADVICE
www.blogstorm.co.uk
www.davidnaylor.co.uk. Search engine optimisation consultant.

THANKS

This book was the result of a teatime conversation with Martin Liu of Marshall Cavendish. I was telling him about a course I was teaching at the University of West London, for entrepreneurs to learn about marketing and getting started online. I was spending a fortune on books because there wasn't one simple, all encompassing publication that could tell them what they needed to know: how to merge their marketing with their online strategy, sit down and get going.

"Why don't you write it?" Martin said. So I did.

Thanks to Martin Liu, all my entrepreneurial business students who asked me questions I had to go away and find answers to, Andrew Day, Duncan Clubb and Dug Falby who did amazing work at Offworld Industries way before the terrestrial population had realised what was happening online, Peter Borg, Mick Casey and Rachel

Moore for keeping me online, Andrew Stibbs and Asato Ohno for teaching me about search engine optimisation, Paul Greeves for getting Lush online very early on, Caroline Walsh for shoving me into the University of West London lecturing job and Nick Randell for pretending to listen to all my ideas, and for listening carefully to the important ones.

Special thanks to Angela Routley for telling me that she was driving along the coned-off section of the information superhighway. I borrowed her phrase. This book is for her, Mary Linehan, John Simmons and all my other friends who have asked me to explain how to approach the world of online marketing.

Thanks, too, to all the entrepreneurial spirits, people who are busy running their own businesses, who filled in my survey and sent me their recommendations, views and opinions about their own online marketing. (If I've made any mistakes, it's not their fault.)

- Pete Cornes. www.pilcrow.com.uk. Outstanding copywriter.

- Tony Rowlands. www.ajrowlands.com. My most excellent accountant.

- Ally Hill. www.sarva.co.uk. Inspiring yoga teacher and co-owner of the Sarva yoga centre.

- Sarah McCartney (no relation). www.symmetrycounselling.com. Counsellor.

- Lucie Gray. www.facebook.com/lucie.gray. Designer.

- Emma Runciman. http://thinksaydo.co.uk. Researcher and K1squirt kayak champion.

- Jo Larney. www.jolarneyphotography.com. Wedding and lifestyle photographer.

- Claire Carroll. www.clairelouisecarroll.com, www.beefencounter.com. Actor and writer.

- Chas Walton. www.textwizard.com. Copywriter.

- Lorelei Mathias. www.loreleimathias.com. Copywriter and novelist.

- Sarah Pierce. www.pierceparryassociates.co.uk, www.merchantsofvino.com. HR and career consultant and part-time wine merchant.

- Rick Senley. www.ricksenley.com. Photojournalist.

- Anna Penrose. www.mail-away.co.uk. Email marketer.

- Peter Borg. www.restaurantelosroques.com. Webmaster and restaurateur.

- Rachel Moore. www.digitalangels.co.uk. Web designer.

- Joseph and Elizabeth Pritchard. www.zeteticmind. com. Strategic business miracle-workers.

- Andrew Stibbs. www.steamcream.com. Web designer and marketer.

- Alex McCartney-Moore. www.guitarlute.co.uk. Musician and restorer.

ABOUT THE AUTHOR

Sarah McCartney wrote her MA dissertation on online marketing in 1996 when less than 1% of the UK population had internet access. Working with some astonishingly intelligent uber-geeks and visionaries, at this time she probably knew more about the subject than anyone else in London for about three weeks. Then the rest of the world caught up. Since that time, she has been working with businesses to make sure that what they do online helps them to build their brands and give their customers what they need. After teaching a course on internet marketing at her local university in 2010, and reading far too many books on the subject, she decided that none of them really did the job. This is the result.

You can find Sarah's writing website at www.littlemax. co.uk and her creativity website at www.4160Tuesdays. com. Please drop in and say hello.